STOCK MARKET TRADING
FOR BEGINNERS

Everything You Need to Know to Start
Investing and Make Money in the Stock Market

David Morales

TABLE OF CONTENTS

INTRODUCTION

This book is intended for people who have already decided to invest in the stock market. You have already decided that you're going to invest in a particular asset class: stocks. You have already compared the stock market's performance and stock investing with other ways of growing your savings like real estate, art collecting or bonds.

To recap, you have probably made this decision for the following reasons. First, stocks are liquid. Unlike real estate, which can take quite some time to sell off, you can quickly sell your stock assets at any time. There is always a ready group of people waiting to buy your stock. This market is not going to go away. The stock market, after all, is a global market. There is absolutely no waiting involved.

Despite all these advantages you might not get the price that you want when you sell your shares-, still, when you compare stock trading with real estate, you can still end up ahead with stocks. Not only do you run the risk of not getting the price you want for your real estate assets, but you might also have to wait a long time to unload them. At least with stocks, only one of these disadvantages is present. Indeed, in many cases, there are no disadvantages at all.

The reason why stocks are so liquid is because the market for stocks is a global market. It's made up of millions of ready buyers and sellers. We're not talking about people that are waiting to be notified of a stock auction or who are on some sort of buyers' list. We're not talking about some sort of time lag before they get the notification. Instead, these are people who are already in the market and are ready to snap up shares quickly as they are made available at any given time. Of course, buyers have to think the price is right.

On top of individual buyers and sellers, there's also an abundance of market makers. These are brokerage firms and finance companies that make it their business to buy and hold stocks for eventual resale. Alternatively, they also have control over certain stocks they can buy and sell readily.

Another advantage of stocks is real time valuation. Again, there's no need to wait here. Unlike other asset classes like art or real estate or collectibles like comic books, you don't have to wait for an appraisal. You don't have to wait for the latest auction to set up some sort of threshold price range. Instead, you only need to look up the stock price of the company that you're interested in buying to see the real time price of the stock.

The price, of course, is established by factoring in the bid and asks prices for that stock. The higher the volume of shares being traded in real time, the less the difference between bid and ask prices. Still, you get a tremendous advantage with real time pricing because there's no guesswork involved. There's no waiting. There's no hoping that the market is hot enough to adequately price your shares. The market is always available and ready to buy your shares. Again, it might not be the price that you want, but you can easily access the real time price of your stock.

Just as importantly, the stock price is very active. In other words, it responds in real time to supply and demand. You're not dealing with some sort of "official" price where it's anybody's guess what the real price is. Instead, you see the actual state of demand for certain shares at any given time.

Next, market value tends to increase over time. While there are no guarantees in life-and this is definitely the case with investments-generally speaking, stocks beat inflation year after year. If you're taking a broad view of stock valuation, let' say a 20-year or even a 30-year period, you can bet that it would beat inflation. This is a big deal.

How come Inflation?

Inflation eats up the value of your hard earned money over time. With each passing year, the amount of goods and services you could buy with $100 decreases. As recently as 50 years ago, 10 cents can actually buy a lot of things. In fact, a few hundred dollars would be enough to buy a house. That's right, a complete house! Good luck renting a house with that same amount nowadays.

Inflation kills the value of your money. As time goes by, you need more and more money to buy the same amount of stuff and services. The worst part to all of this is that inflation will continue to impact your finances long in the future. It's not going to stop or disappear.

Currently, we're living in a low inflation environment. This hasn't always been the case. There were a few relatively long periods in American history where inflation hit double digits.

It's anybody's guess when those bad times will happen again. When inflation soars, the value of goods and services you can buy with your money decreases tremendously.

Stocks have historically been a good hedge against inflation. By ensuring that your money grows at a higher rate than inflation, you offset whatever damage to your money's value inflation inflicts. This is one of the main reasons why people invest in stocks and real estate in the first place. They need a way of preserving, as much as possible, the value of their hard-earned money.

Congratulations!

Congratulations if you have decided to take action now because, in all likelihood, if you get into the market now, the value of your holdings will be worth more in 5 to 10 years or more. The longer your time horizon, the higher the appreciation of your investment portfolio's value.

The sooner you invest, the longer you stretch your investment time horizon, it's more likely compounding would benefit you. In other words, your money would appreciate and that appreciated value would, in turn, appreciate some more. For example, if you buy stocks that pay dividends, the longer you hang on to these stocks while automatically reinvesting your dividends, the higher the likelihood your holdings' value will increase over time.

Also, by investing now, you may be able to take advantage of stock opportunities that are present now which may not be as attractive as when you kept on waiting to enter the market. I remember when I first got into stock investing, around that time, Microsoft's stock started splitting. I think I started monitoring Microsoft after its first two stock splits. Imagine the tremendous opportunities present at that time.

If you were able to pick up shares of Microsoft when they were priced very low, you could be very wealthy now. The same applies to current stocks like Netflix or Google. Imagine buying Microsoft or Apple Computer when they were still attractively priced.

No wonder a lot of people jump into the stock market to lock in on hot stocks that are priced at attractive price per earnings ratios. These P/E ratios may not persist for long. It's a good idea to get started with stock investing as early as possible.

I understand that you're excited. I understand that you probably can't wait to get going, but let me tell you, before you jump in, you need to get the basics right. Before you roll up your sleeves and start putting your money to work with your stock investments, you need to make sure understand the basics of stock investing. Otherwise, it's too easy to screw up. Seriously.

You worked hard for your money. You made a lot of sacrifices, and it really would be a shame to jeopardize all of that because you did not lay the proper foundation as far as your research and stock selection strategy are concerned.

Please understand that the more time you invest in properly studying stock investing, the higher the likelihood that you would actually become profitable.

Who is This Book For?

This book is for people who see the value of stock investing but don't know the fundamentals yet. They don't know the nitty-gritty basics of stock investing.

Now, let me be clear, this book is not intended for intermediate or expert investors. This book is strictly for beginners. With that said, there are certain details in beginner stock investing that you need to wrap your mind around, otherwise, it's too easy to make the wrong decision and end up losing money or sitting on a stock that will continue to trade sideways for a long time to come.

This book is also dedicated to people who are looking to start their stock investing career right. It's easy to start your stock investing adventure the wrong way. You end up blowing through a lot of money. It can involve a lot of expensive learning experiences. This happens to the very best of us.

But the good news is, you don't necessarily have to go through such an expensive learning experience. It is possible to study investing in such a way that you make fewer mistakes in the beginning. In fact, if you are diligent enough, it's possible to start with no mistakes at all. It really all boils down to you.

And this book is dedicated to and aimed at people who are looking to start investing in stocks the right way. Instead of having to find out things in the hardest way possible, why not just get off on the right foot and learn how to do things right the first time around?

What Will This Book Teach You?

This book will teach you the following information. Again, these are the basics that you need to start trading and trade in such a way that decreases your likelihood of losing money.

Your first focus should be on losing as little money as possible. Start there and then move on to making as much money as possible. Believe me, it's much better to do things this way than the other way around.

This book will teach you the following:

- ✓ How is Money Made in the Stock Market?
- ✓ Setting Yourself Up to Start Trading
- ✓ How Investors Pick Stocks to Trade
- ✓ The Basics of Fundamental Investing
- ✓ The Basics of Technical Trading
- ✓ Identifying and Picking the Right Growth Stocks
- ✓ Identifying and Picking the Right Income Stocks
- ✓ Picking an Investing Strategy that Suits You
- ✓ How to Research Stocks
- ✓ Pooled Investments: Are They Right for You?

CHAPTER 1:

HOW IS MONEY MADE IN THE STOCK MARKET?

When you're buying stocks, you are essentially buying ownership in the company that issued that stock. When you buy a share of Alphabet Inc (Google's parent company) stock, you are legally buying a unit of ownership in that company. You have become an owner of the search engine that you use every single day.

Of course, with ownership comes rights. That chunk of the company that you own can be bought and sold. That is the asset that you are investing in. While some companies do give you a cut of the profits that it makes every single year, not all companies do this.

When you buy or sell stock, please understand that there's always two sides to a transaction. There's always a buyer and a seller. The seller or buyer may not always be an individual. It can be an institution like a mutual fund. It can be a retirement pension fund. It can even be a governmental agency operating a sovereign fund. It can take many different forms. But the bottom line is that they are putting up money to buy shares or they are holding stock for eventual sale. They paid money for that stock earlier.

Keep this in mind because a lot of newbie stock investors think that when they buy and sell stock, they're essentially betting against the house. They think there's some sort of giant bank or some sort of large institution at the other end. This is not the case. You can be buying from another individual or you can be buying from a small institution. There's a wide range of individuals and institutions you can buy from, but stock trading always involves buying and selling.

Keep in mind that stock trading primarily involves the secondary market. Unlike an IPO where you buy the stock directly from the company, the stock that you buy and sell on the stock market has already been issued to the public. The shares you're buying probably have changed hands many times before. For you to get shares, somebody has to sell them.

Wins and Losses are Relative

Of course, whenever there's some sort of exchange involved, it's natural to think of winning and losing. It's natural to think that if you bought shares at a low price and eventually unload it for a higher price, the person that you bought it from is the loser. Similarly, if you bought a stock at a high price and have basically given up on the stock appreciating so you sell it after it has crashed, it's easy to think that you have lost out. This is all relative. It really all boils down to timing. You only lose out when you sell for a price lower than the price you paid for your shares.

You might be thinking that, when it's time to unload a stock because you feel that it's just going to trade sideways forever, you're actually winning. You're getting rid of an asset that you think is hopeless (at least for the short term).

On the other hand, the buyer thinks they're winning because they are buying at a price that's attractive to them. In other words, they think stock that it would appreciate at some point in time. Even if you were to sell a stock at a much higher price than you originally bought for it, the buyer might still think he or she is a winner.

It's obvious that you would think you're a winner because if you paid only $10 for a stock and you're unloading it at $50, you're making $40 per share. What if you bought thousands of shares? You're coming out a big time winner. Well, believe it or not, the buyer can think he or she is coming out ahead as well. They're buying at a price that's attractive to them because they think the stock would continue to go up. Both of you are winning at that point.

Even if you are selling the stock at a loss, as I mentioned earlier, you can still think that you're coming out ahead. If you have given up hope on the stock, you might be thinking that you're gaining because you're cutting your losses before the stock's performance worsens further. It really all boils down to perspective. A seller may be relieved to unload a stock or is cashing out a gain. A buyer, on the other hand, regardless of the price, feels like he or she is a winner because they obviously think that the stock will appreciate further.

The Only Way to Make Money on the Stock Market

With all the differences in points of view outlined above, keep in mind that there is only one way to make money on the stock market: buy low and sell high. This is the classic definition of "long trading." You buy and you wait for the stock price to go up and you get rid of the stock. You lock in on the difference between the lower price you bought it for and the higher price you exited at.

This can happen fairly quickly. There are fast rising stocks in any given day that can appreciate 1%, 2%, 5% or even more than 10%. Imagine buying a stock in the morning at $10 and after a couple of hours, exiting the stock at $12. You made 20% for the day. If you were to multiply that $10 by thousands of shares, you can see the big money involved here. And it all materialized in the span of a few hours!

Alternatively, you can buy stock at a fairly low price and wait weeks, months or even years until you decide to let it go at a much higher price. It really all depends on you and your time frame. It depends on how much the stock appreciated.

Short Selling Stocks

Interestingly enough, there is another way to make money off the stock market, but it doesn't violate the rule of buying low and selling high. This alternative is called a short sale. You probably heard this form of trading before. You sell a stock when it's trading high, and then when it crashes, you buy it back at a much lower rate. The profit, of course, is the difference between the prices you sold it for and how much you bought it back to cover your bet. Believe it or not, you're still engaged in buying low and selling high. You just reversed the process.

The reason why this is even possible is because market makers like brokerages actually control large amounts of stock. When you sell a stock short at a high price, you essentially borrow the stock from a market maker and dump it. You wait for the price to crash, and then you cover your short sale by buying the shares back, the difference is your profit.

Why sell stocks short? The main reason why there is such an active short sale market is because stocks often rise slowly. In many cases, they trade sideways.

For example, you bought a stock for $10 and it takes a whole year for it to go to $10.50. For pretty much the whole year, it doesn't really break out all that much. It stays within a narrow range and the long term trend line for that stock's price is an appreciation of 50 cents over the course of a year. This is how the majority of stocks behave-on the upside.

However, when they experience turbulence or there are problems with the company, they don't track sideways. Instead, they move in a more direct way. They drop. For people looking to make money off the stock market in a shorter period of time or who are looking for more active action for their investments, short sales make a lot of sense. If news came out that a company's having problems achieving profitability or they missed an earnings estimate, there might be a tremendous downward pressure on the stock price. It would be easier for you to make money off a stock that is dropping than one that is tracking sideways for a year.

Options are Not Immune to the Classic Rule of Stock Investing

Even stock options are not exceptions to the rule listed above on how to make money with stocks. When you buy an option, you're essentially just given a right to take certain action over a fixed amount of stocks. However, buying such rights don't also mean you have an obligation to take such action. In other words, when you buy an option, you are given the right to buy or sell, but you're not forced to buy or sell the stock by a certain date. Options are exactly that-they are options. They are actions that you may or may not want to take.

There are two types of options. Options that give you a right to buy at a certain price, and options that give you a right to sell at a certain price. These are strategic options.

When you buy an option that gives you the right to buy at a certain price, this is called a call option. And naturally, the right that you are buying is to pick up shares at a low price. The reverse is also true. You can buy options that give you the right to sell at a certain price, and this price is going to be higher than the price of the stock at the time you're going to exercise the option. This is called a put option.

The bottom line with options is that they protect your position depending on where you think the stock's price is headed. Put options protect your investment if you think the stock price is going to sink. Similarly, if you think that stock prices are going to go up, you lock in your gains through a call option.

All this may sound amazing and everything, but you have to understand that when you are buying an option, you pay a premium for that option. You're paying for the right to buy or sell at a certain price. You not only have to pay for the right, but you also have to pay for the stock if you're going to be buying it. The bottom line is that options enable you to earn off a stock's value while paying only a small portion of the full stock price. The options themselves are valuable because you can buy the option at a fraction of the actual value of the underlying stock itself.

As mentioned above, options are not immune to the iron rule of stock trading. You still have to buy low and sell high if you want to make a profit. The only twist that option trading brings to the table is the protection based on the underlying stock price, but the same dynamic still applies. It's all about buying low and making money when the value rises to create a profit margin.

What Makes Stock Prices Go Up?

Now that we are clear as to how people make money off the stock market, let's get to the heart of the action. We need to wrap our minds around two central questions: What exactly are people betting on? Why do stock prices go up and down?

Stock prices really all boil down to public perception. This is the most accurate driver of stock prices... A lot of newbie investors automatically think that a stock's price goes up and down primarily due to the performance and quality of the underlying company. Well, you can be forgiven for thinking that because that's a very logical and well-reasoned conclusion. Reasonable people think that way.

The problem is, the market may not agree. A company's stock price is essentially a judgment on its current earnings and predicted future earnings growth. The price is just an opinion offered by the stock market in general. It's not necessarily a reflection of the company's actual fundamentals.

In fact, there are many companies that have very little debt, have high book-value, are solid industry players, and are going places. They also possess tremendous industry. Still, their stock is not performing as well as heavily-hyped and extremely popular stocks like Tesla or Facebook. What gives? What's going on?

Well, again, the stock price is not necessarily about the fundamentals of the company. Instead, a stock's price gauges the opinion that the stock market has on that stock's potential and immediate prospects. In other words, it's about market popularity.

What if I told you that Tesla actually makes most of its money through government alternative energy subsidies? When it comes to head to head comparison with more established auto makers, like Ford, Tesla actually doesn't compare all that well. Still, Tesla stock is Wall Street's darling. There are also smaller tech companies whose stocks are just blowing up, but their fundamentals are an embarrassment compared to larger more established industry players.

Do you see how this works?

Market popularity and market trends count for a lot. There is a tendency for stocks to become popular or less popular based on market trends. For example, in a given quarter, if utility stocks become trendy among hedge fund managers, mutual fund directors and other institutional buyers, you can bet that, on average, those types of stocks will go up in value. Now, if they fall out of favor the next quarter, the reverse can also true. Everybody will start dumping those stocks and, right or wrong, those stocks are in the dog house in terms of pricing. None of this has any impact on these companies' overall financial fitness and performance.

When looking to buy stocks, understand that it's not just about the fundamentals of the company. While fundamentals go a long way because there's a big difference between a company making a profit and a company that's bleeding red, there's a lot more going on. There's a lot more factors that you need to take account of when determining how well a company's stock will probably perform.

Keep in mind that there are often solid companies that are overlooked by the stock market. There are also junk companies that are just very trendy and don't really offer much value which are bid up ridiculously by the market. The bottom line is simple: markets are driven by emotions. When it comes to the global stock market, there really are only two emotions that you need to pay attention to: fear and greed.

As the old saying goes, buy when everyone's fearful, sell when everyone's getting greedy. Keep this is mind because these two emotions are the primary drivers of stock prices. They can either pump stock prices up, or they can push them down. And in many cases, all that action has little to do with the actual meat and potatoes of the companies behind those shares.

How Do You Make Money Off a Stock?

To recap, how do you make money off a stock you buy and sell? You can make money by buying low, and then holding it until it increases in value. This is called long trading.

You can borrow stock when it's trading at a high price and then sell the stock. You wait for the price to drop quite a bit, and then you buy back those shares to cover the stock you borrowed. This is called short trading.

You make money, of course, in the difference between the price you initially sold the stock for, and the price you eventually bought the stock to cover your initial investment. This process still involves the classic rule of buying low and selling high, just in reverse.

You also make money from stocks when you buy companies that split their profits with shareholders. This distributed profit is called a dividend. The shares of companies who distribute dividends regularly are called income stocks. There are a large number of these. These are usually utilities and energy companies.

You can also make money off a stock when it splits. For example, a company may not give dividends, but you can still make quite a bit of money from that company when it splits its stock and you sell off the additional stock. There are many companies that split two to one, two to three, in some cases, even three to one.

For example, you begin with one share and the company announces a three for one split. If you paid $30 for that one share, you will have 3 shares after the split. Each share is valued at $10 usually, companies split their stocks when they think that the stock price is so high that the high value is getting in the way of other investors properly bidding up the stock price. Alternatively, some companies view stock splits as an alternative to issuing dividends to their shareholders.

CHAPTER 2:
SETTING YOURSELF UP TO START TRADING

Now that you have a clear idea of how money is made on the stock market and what stocks are, the next step is to set up the tools that you need so you can start trading and start making money. Keep in mind that this involves more than just filling out online forms.

It's easy to start an online trading account nowadays because almost all brokers have websites that enable you to trade online. Opening the account is not the issue. The bigger issue is whether you've done enough thinking as to the type of account you want to start.

This is very important because it's very easy to think that if you've picked one broker on one account, you've pretty much picked them all because they are essentially all the same. This is the kind of thinking that could lead you to making some serious mistakes down the road. You might end up positioning yourself to lose money unnecessarily.

You have to be clear from the beginning about the type of objectives you have, your risk appetite, your age factor and other important considerations. These determine which type of broker you're going to go with, what level of management you're going to sign up for and other important details that play a big role in whether you would achieve the kind of success you're looking for. This is not something to be undertaken lightly. You have to do some advanced thinking here. You have to think ahead.

What Do You Need to Start Trading Stocks in the United States?

First of all, you need to pick a US-based broker. This is an online trading platform that is based in the United States and registered with the SEC of the United States government. The SEC regulates exchanges which in turn regulates online brokers. You have to open an account with an online trading platform that has a formal relationship with the NASDAQ and other trading markets as well as official recognition from the US government.

The good news is that all online brokers in the United States are already in compliance with these regulations. They have to unless they cannot operate legally. The trickier issue is to determine which type of broker you're going to with.

Picking Your Type of Broker

You might be thinking to yourself that since all online trading platforms pretty much function the same way, that they are essentially one and the same. You would be absolutely wrong. There is a big difference between a full-service broker and a discount broker. You can tell from their very categorization ("full service" versus "discount") that there is quite a bit of difference as far as service offerings are concerned.

The Benefits of a Full-Service Broker

When you open an account with a full-service brokerage firm, you're not on your own. You're not going to be planning your own stock trades. You're not going to just do your research by yourself. You're going to get a tremendous amount of guidance, advice, and recommendations.

In fact, a lot of full-service brokerage firms have distinguished themselves in giving out stock trading and stock purchase advice that have made their clients quite wealthy. The more spot-on they are in their advice and recommendations, the stronger their firm's reputation becomes.

As you can tell, they have a vested interest in making sure that they make the right calls more often than not. Accordingly, a lot of full-service brokerages invest quite a bit of resources in analysts as well as professional stock pickers to ensure that their advice and recommendation by enlarge beat the market or at least draw favorable attention to the brokerage. They spend a lot of resources finding the right talent. They have to-people who have a knack for picking winning stocks consistently don't come cheap!

With that said, please keep in mind that there are possible conflicts of interest here. Many brokerages do take a position in the companies that they are promoting. I hope you can see the conflict here. If a company is going to materially benefit from a stock that they are actively promoting, there is a temptation to push the stock even if there might be better alternatives out there. This is the risk that you run.

The good news? The US government has put in place all sorts of safeguards to ensure that, at the very least, the investing public, meaning you, have a way to know whether there are potential conflicts. By law, your full-service brokerage, if they have an analyst or recommendation, must disclose whatever interest they may have in whatever stocks they are promoting or recommending.

You Get Tremendous Research Materials

Another great benefit of going with a full-service broker is that you get access to a wide range of research materials. Now, you may be thinking that you really don't need this if you are already going to be taking their advice or recommendations regarding specific stocks. Not necessarily.

If you want to cross-reference whatever recommendations they come up with, you would need access to a wide range of materials to help you make sure that the stocks you think are hot are actually backed up by facts and proven financial information. You increase your likelihood of finding this information if you have access to a wide range of research materials provided by your full-service broker. It doesn't really matter whether they directly researched such materials or got these from another source.

Investment Planning Services

Full-service brokerages also give you advice on how to plan your investment. They first look at your age, your assets and your goals. They then craft together a workable financial planning strategy that would position you to invest in such a way that grows your assets over an expected timeline.

Now, this isn't a slam dunk. Nobody can guarantee how the economy would perform in the future. Nobody could guarantee how well the stock market would in the future.

With that said, with solid investment planning, you increase your chances of benefiting and prospering as the greater American and global economy prospers. At the very least, you don't stand the risk of being left behind when things change directions or there are tremendous opportunities in the market. Going with a full-service broker's investment planning services enables you to get well-positioned to take advantage of favorable changes in the investment landscape.

They Trade for You

Most importantly, when you go with the full-service brokerage, they make the trades for you. You can set up all sorts of conditions, and they would follow your conditions while trading your stocks. This decreases the likelihood that you would make a mistake. This also increases the likelihood that you may lock in at the most favorable prices.

Of course, this doesn't guarantee anything. The market moves really quickly. It changes directions rapidly. Still, when you have expert guidance in making trades, this increases the likelihood that you would get the results that you are looking for.

The Drawbacks of Full-Service Brokerages

Of course, nothing in life is completely free of disadvantages. There are always pros and cons to everything. This definitely applies to full-service brokerages.

First of all, you're going to pay a lot more money with full-service brokerages. Somebody has to pay for the wide range of services as well as managed trading and planning that they offer. You would be that person. You get more services so you have to pay for those services compared to discount brokers.

The next disadvantage of going with a full-service broker is the sales orientation of their recommendations and stock picks. While you are still the final decision maker as to whether you are going to go with these recommendations, you might feel quite a bit of pressure due to the trust you have developed for your broker

Whenever you start to trust somebody, and they make all sorts of recommendations, there's always the possibility that there may be a conflict of interest. As mentioned above, there many brokerages do have research arms that also recommend stocks that the company has a vested interest in.

The good news is that you can read the disclaimers that come with their research and recommendations. Factor that in into your ultimate decision.

Benefits of a Discount Broker

There are many platforms up n the Internet that just enable you to buy and sell securities. That's pretty much all they do since these "barebones" and extremely basic trading platforms are stripped free of any frills. You can rest assured that they can help you trade at the cheapest rate possible. We're talking about less than $10 a trade regardless how many shares you buy and regardless of the value of the stock you trade.

Now, compare this with full-service brokerages which often index the cost you pay for the trade to the value of the stocks that you are buying or selling. It may seem like it's a fairly small amount in the beginning, but it actually adds up especially if you scale up your trades.

You don't have any of those problems when you're dealing with a discount broker. You get cheap, straight, across-the-board low rates. Additionally, you get full control. There is no pesky or pushy salesperson trying to impress on you a particular stock or trying to draw your attention to supposedly "hot" stocks that have "a lot of potential."

You're completely free of any of that kind of stress and pressure. You are in full control of your trades. You only have yourself to blame if things go wrong, and you only have yourself to thank if things go right.

Moreover, you get the benefit of quick execution. One hassle with full-service brokers is that there is sometimes a lag between your decision to trade and the actual execution.

While they do a good job in executing the trade once they get your order, sometimes there is this lag on your end

With discount brokers, you don't have a lag. You just log on and do the orders yourself. It's that quick and easy. Think. Trade. Easy as 1-2-3.

Now, don't get too excited. Depending on the volume of trading involving the stock, there might be so many people trying to exit or enter the stock that there might be some time before your particular order is executed. We're talking possibly between seconds and minutes. Sometimes, it can take quite a while if the volume is really high.

Please understand that this problem is not going to go away regardless of how much you trade unless you're one of the biggest institutional traders out there. Everybody has to fall in line and this includes electronic trading.

The Drawbacks of Discount Brokers

The biggest drawback to using a cheap online discount broker to trade stocks in the United States and elsewhere is the fact that they assume that you know what you're doing. There's nobody there to hold your hand. There's nobody there to tell you to reconsider regarding potential trades.

You are pretty much assumed to know what you're doing, and you will be treated like an adult meaning if it's obvious that you are going to be trading badly, nobody's going to tap your hand and tell you to take it easy. Instead, you are allowed to go ahead and trade because nobody's watching.

The assumption is you know full well what you're getting into, you take the blame if things go south or the credit when things go right.

Another assumption that proves to be a drawback of discount brokers involves prior research. The broker platform assumes that you've done your homework. There's no need for discount broker-supplied researched recommendations because it's assumed you already know what you are getting into.

Keep in mind that many higher-value discount brokers do offer free research services, but they are quite limited compared to full-range or full-service brokers. In fact, their platforms are often so stripped bare of the extras that you basically have to buy a third-party service if you want stock research that is fairly robust.

I'm not saying that you're not getting any value from the free tools made available to you by discount brokers, but you shouldn't have high expectations. At the very least, you'll just get basic information. In some cases, there's some delay in the info but considering the fact that it's absolutely free, the old rule of beggars can't be choosers definitely applies in this situation.

Finally, as cheap as discount brokers may appear on the surface, please understand that there are still possible hidden charges. It's a good idea to ask the discount broker for their full schedule of fees. Make sure you are completely aware of what potential charges may appear in the future.

Don't get blindsided. Don't assume that just because you're paying less than $10 a trade that your costs are set in stone. There might be other things going on with your trade where you might inadvertently trigger these other charges.

By law, broker platforms are required to share this information with you. They cannot hide the ball but unfortunately, most people simply just breeze through the fine print on online forms when making trades. They only have themselves to blame when they get surprised by 'hidden' charges. Don't be one of those people.

Check the complete schedule of rates posted on the online trading platform. They may initially buried in the fine print, but the discount broker is legally required to give you a clear, easy-to-understand explanation of the rates or, at the very least, a presentation of how to the rates stack up and what events trigger them.

Whatever You Do, Do These

Before you decide on whether to go with a discount broker or a full-service broker, you must first wrap your mind around your investing goals. What exactly are you trying to accomplish?

For example, if you have $100,000 in the bank that you'd like to grow into $500,000 by the time you retire, stocks are probably a good vehicle for that, but you can also try real state. Certain real-estate markets in the United States are red hot. They can remain warm during economic downturns and when the economy recovers, they get even hotter.

However, it really all depends on your investing goals as well as your timelines. You have to have a clear strategy as to what you want to do with your investment capital so you're not surprised later.

Your choice of broker, whether it's a discount broker or a full-service broker, must fit your investing goals. You must either get the guidance you need to achieve these goals, or you need a powerful platform that would enable you to trade independently and quickly so you can get one step closer to achieving your goals.

Furthermore, you need to be clear on the fees, charges and rates that they have. This goes without saying, but you have to take the initiative. Don't think that just because it's buried in the fine print, you'll get to it when you have the time. Wrong attitude. Chances are you would end up paying more than you need to.

You have to take the first step and be proactive to ensure that you are as clear as possible as to what these charges are because they do eat into your gains and compound your losses.

Opening the Right Type of Account

Please keep in mind that there are different account options out there whether you go with a discount broker or a full-service broker. There to main account types - cash and margin.

If you have discipline issues, or you just want to make sure that you steer clear of going into debt, opening a cash account makes a lot of sense in your situation. With this account, you can only trade the amount of cash you have on hand. You cannot extend your cash balance through credit.

This may seem pretty straightforward, but you have to factor in commission. Make no mistake about it even if you're using a low-cost discount trader, there are commissions involved. They still have to make money, and they make this amount through their rates and charges. You need to make sure that you have enough cash to cover stock purchases while factoring in commissions.

Margin Accounts

Margin accounts are essentially credit accounts. You deposit a certain minimum amount of cash with your broker. The broker than automatically "extends" your purchasing ability based on the value of the stock you buy with the cash. The stock acts as security for future purchases or short sales.

Keep in mind that this extension of the value of your cash only happens when you purchase stock. The thinking here is that it's the stock that actually guarantees the credit. It's not the actual cash you have. Keep this in mind.

Just because you put in let's say a $100,000 into your account, the act of depositing doesn't magically transform your cash into $200,000 of stock-purchasing power. It doesn't work that way. You have to take the 100,000 and buy stocks with it and then from there, the total value of the account is extended.

Keep in mind that since this is a credit arrangement with interest charged on a daily basis. Don't drag things out to such an extent that you end up losing money.

The bottom line is if you can't pay your margin, the broker does a margin call and sells off your stock to cover the amount you owe. There are many cases where you end up owing your broker after they have liquidated all your stock. Sounds crazy, right? It happens so do yourself a big favor and make sure that you study what exactly you're getting into if you decide to get a margin account.

Don't get me wrong. Margin accounts can help you, but you have to use them in the right context. Margin accounts are great for making fast purchases to lock in fast-appearing opportunities.

For example, you've already bought Netflix, and your $100,000 is sunk into that stock. It turns out, however, that after a couple of days, Apple Inc stock starts to drop rapidly. Sensing the possibility that the stock will then bounce up with a vengeance, you can borrow against the value of your Netflix stock and buy Apple shares. Once the rally materializes, you can exit the stock, pay off the margin and what's left is your profit. Or you can sell off just enough Apple shares to cover your margin costs and keep the remaining shares as profit.

If you know what you're doing, and you pull this off correctly, you can end up with quite a bit of a gain. Please understand that you have to track your purchases properly; otherwise, your borrowing may get the better of you. You might end up with a margin call because you've spread yourself too thin.

Moreover, you cannot borrow unlimited amounts of money. The margin limit is 50%. This means you can purchase stocks that are 50% more than the value of the underlying stock or cash. For example, if you have $10,000 in cash, you can buy $20,000 worth of securities.

Margin accounts charge interest. I can't repeat this enough. Make sure you factor this in when making a decision selling or cashing out your positions.

Determine Your Stock Trading Objectives

Why are you thinking of trading stocks in the first place? Are you thinking of growing your wealth or preserving it? Similarly, are you thinking of buying assets that would produce income?

Now, it may seem that these objectives are fairly similar to each other since they all involve the stocks of publicly traded companies, but they are actually quite different from each other. Growing wealth is different from preserving wealth as well as getting a nice cash flow. Keep in mind the following discussions.

Are You Trying to Grow Your Wealth?

Ideally, younger people should consider this as their primary stock-trading goal. We're talking about investors who are less than 40 years old. The reason being, you still have enough time to make up for your losses should you make some bad bets. This is harder to do when you're over 40 years old, and you have a house with a mortgage and kids and college expenses to worry about, so on and so forth.

However, if you're just fresh out of college and working at your first real job, you can make a lot of risky bets with growth stocks. These are stocks that may not be making all that much money, but are very popular with the stock market. Even though they may have high stock prices, they may still appreciate further.

The downside with these stocks is things can easily go south or trends may reverse and you may end up with a whole lot of nothing.

If you're young enough you can bounce back and recover.

Unfortunately, if you are more than 40 years old, it's much harder to recover, and you might get wiped out by waiting for a long time as the stock continues to drop or trade sideways.

Are You Trying to Preserve Your Wealth?

People with a wealth preservation goal tend to be older. These are investors who are aged 50-55 years old. As they get closer to retirement age, they are less concerned about growing the value of their investment portfolio than they are with preserving its value.

In other words, their main goal is to beat inflation. As I've mentioned earlier, inflation is the silent killer of wealth. If you were to put all your hard-earned money in the bank and just leave it there, you're going to lose out. If you leave it there long enough, you're going to lose out big.

Why? Inflation. Every single year, the amount of goods and services your money buys, decreases by a certain rate. You have to find a way to grow the value of your money that beats the rate of inflation. You have to also factor in taxes that you have to pay for whatever interest the bank pays you. Given the current low-interest environment, banks aren't paying you much of anything in terms of interest.

Accordingly, people use the stock market as a way to preserve wealth because generally speaking, stocks appreciate at a much higher rate than the rate of inflation. This modest growth compared to growth stocks, is often enough to offset taxes and inflation.

Are You Looking for Income from Your Stock Holdings?

A third class of investors is looking for income. Basically, they buy stocks and they benefit from the appreciation of the underlying stock price as well as the dividend payout of that stock. In other words, these companies will pay you a certain percentage of their income every single year.

These are great because you win on two levels. You win when the value of the stock increases. You also win because every year, you get a certain amount of dollars for every share of that company stock.

If this sounds awesome to you, you might want to hold back because there are definite disadvantages with income stocks as well. They sound great, but the picture is actually a little more complicated than you realize.

CHAPTER 3:

HOW INVESTORS PICK STOCKS TO TRADE?

By this point, you have set up your accounts and you're clear as to what your initial stock profile and objectives are. You should also have a fairly clear idea of whether you're trying to grow or preserved wealth or whether you're looking for income from your stock holdings.

The next step is to determine how you're going to go pick your stocks. This is extremely important because your stock picks determine your success. Pick a dog, and you're not going to make money and possibly lose money. Pick an eagle or a dragon and you stand to make quite a bit of money over the long haul.

Making stock picks are actually done in one of four ways

First, you can trade using the recommendations of brokers' analysts and research departments. These are highly paid people who know the stock market quite well. They are experts in their field and, generally, their recommendations come with quite a bit of trust because they are the experts in stock trading and stock analysis.

With that said, nobody's perfect. In fact, it's not uncommon for stock analysts to get all excited about a particular stock only to see those shares trade sideways at best. Actually, some get excited about a stock, and the stock eventually tanks. These things do happen. However, by and large, analysts do tend to make the right call. Unfortunately, they might recommend a stock only after it has already risen quite a bit in price. By the time you start trading it, it might already be trading close to its fullest potential.

You can also pick stocks by reading all sorts of stock trading blogs or checking out newspapers or online news reports issued by stock-trading companies. If you've ever watched Bloomberg or CNBC, there is no shortage of stock experts talking about a new discovery regarding a stock that may break out in the future. They talk about companies that are poised to enjoy tremendous growth in the future.

Again, the same warning applies to these people as the analyst research departments of large brokerages. While they can and do often make the right call, they also tend to screw up from time to time. It really would hurt if you only pick up on their bad advice and ignore their good picks. Unfortunately, that's the risk you have to take unless you do your own research to cross reference whatever recommendations they come up with.

The third way to pick stock involves professional managers. You basically put your money that they manage directly. These are mutual funds. They do everything for you. They would do the research. They would do the cross references. They would do the trading.

Additionally, they trade on a very professional way. They don't just jump in. They often buy into a stock in small blocks. They also time their exit from the stock to maximize their gain. Again, these are expert traders who make it his or her life's work to study certain stocks and make the right decisions so you end up gaining a profit.

Unfortunately, just because they've had some success in the past doesn't necessarily mean that success will automatically translate into future excellence. Mutual fund managers, just like any other financial industry experts, can and do screw up from time to time. You have to factor this is in as well.

Finally, you can pick stocks yourself. Thanks to your own direct personal research and your own analysis, you can determine which stocks are worth buying and which ones to ignore. Of course, you can get assistance from the full-service brokerage that you have an account with, or you can just trade directly using a cheap online discount broker.

Quick Notes on Solo Trading

If you're going to be trading on your own, please keep in mind the following. When trading solo, you can trade stocks in two ways. You can simply copy an index, or you can pick individual stocks.

Both of these have their own set of advantages and disadvantages. The great thing about index trading is that you just need to copy and paste the stocks listed for that index.

There's not much thinking involved in picking out the individual stocks. While there's a lot of analysis that would be required in picking which index to follow, as far as the actual stocks are concerned, this is a simple copy and paste job. This can help you save quite a bit of time; however, you have to make sure that you've done your research as far as the feasibility of the specific index you are trading.

Individual Stock Trading

The alternative to index trading is trading individual stocks. You research specific stocks to trade. You figure out their advantages and disadvantages. You make educated predictions about their future performance, and you fit all of this information into your goals and strategies.

Once you're clear that the particular stock fits your budget as well as your goals, you then buy it using a discount online trading platform. Please note that the bulk of this book concentrates on how you can pick individual stocks to trade. We don't really devote a tremendous amount of space to mutual fund investing or full-service brokerage investing since we assume that you're going to be the person who's going to determine which stocks you're going to be trading.

Your First Step

To determine which stocks you're going to be trading on a solo basis, you need to first determine your objectives. Again, are you trying to preserve wealth or grow it? Are you looking to earn an income from your stocks, or are you just going to trade stocks expecting the income to come when you buy low and sell high.

Wealth Preservation

If you're thinking of buying stocks to simply preserve your wealth against inflation, you need to go conservative. The good news is that there are conservative companies out there with solid fundamentals. You can buy blue chip index stocks with solid fundamentals. These are industry leaders. These are companies that are not going anytime soon.

However, the conservative distribution of your investment portfolio must allocate only 20% to stocks. That's it. That's the maximum amount you should invest in stocks.

Eighty percent of your wealth should be in bonds or government securities. These are investment vehicles that guarantee a payout. These are loans from the government and private companies. They have to pay these unless, of course, they're going through bankruptcy. You have to stick to this conservative split. Only 20% of your money should go to stocks and, of those stocks all of them must be blue chip index stocks that are that are very conservative.

Growing Your Wealth

If you are looking to grow your wealth instead of simply protecting it from inflation, you should devote most of your investment portfolio to stocks. We're talking about an 80% distribution. This is the exact opposite of a conservative approach.

Twenty percent of your stocks must be conservative while the remaining 80% should be in aggressive growth stocks. These are more speculative stocks. These produce gains not in terms of dividends, but in terms of stock price. You buy them low and then you sell them for a much higher price. The remaining 20% of your investment portfolio should be restricted to bonds.

Income Generation

If you are looking for stocks that generate enough to get generate cash flow or income, you should companies that pay dividends. The higher the dividend, the better; however, you have to offset this with the underlying price of the stock paying that dividend.

Quick Stock Trading Strategy Overview

You have several choices of strategies when picking stocks to trade. Here's a quick overview. We will drill down into these in more details later. In fact, fundamental investing and technical trading have their own dedicated chapters. My intention with this is to simply give you a quick overview.

When picking stocks to trade, keep in mind that there are many strategies you can pursue. You could do fundamental trading and pick stocks based on how much money they're making now, and how they will probably do in the future.

The whole point of fundamental trading is to find stocks that are not presently appreciated by the stock market. Remember it's all a popularity game. There are great companies that have tremendous potential and are consistent money makers that the stock market, for some reason or other, simply won't reward with a high stock price.

Your job is to size up these companies based on their fundamentals by asking some key questions. How much money do they owe? How big are they in their industries? Do they have great products in the pipeline? How well are they managed? Ask these and other similar questions so you can identify critical variables which will enable you to pick out "Best of Breed" companies. These are well-positioned to eventually be recognized by the stock market in the future. When that happens, expect their stock prices to appreciate.

It all boils down to unlocking potential earnings of the company that may not already be reflected in the company's current stock price.

Quick Note about Warren Buffett

Warren Buffett is one of the world's richest men. In fact, he's always in the Top 10 Forbes List of the World's Wealthiest Individuals. Warren Buffet made his money not by working for somebody else or building a company but investing. He is also the poster child of fundamental analysis. He's all about finding stocks that are currently undervalued by the market.

He has revealed in interview after interview that when he looks at stocks of companies, he moves to buy the companies. He doesn't really care all that much about whether the stock price will go up or down. Instead, he wants to own the company and be part of that company's future income growth. He doesn't really care whether the market will realize the value of the company or not.

Instead, he zeroes in on actual revenue growth.

Sounds good so far, right? Sounds amazing. After all, fundamental analysis definitely paid off for Warren Buffett and investors who follow his strategy.

Unfortunately, as mentioned earlier, everything has an advantage and a disadvantage. While it's easy to see the pros of this approach, there are also cons involved. The big pro is that you get decades of solid results. These companies are less prone to popularity contests, and you lock in on companies that don't suffer from "analyst bias."

The stock market, as mentioned earlier, is a popularity contest. Hot stocks or darling stocks go up in value almost overnight. They're not making a profit. There's a lot of hype surrounding them, but people bid up their stock prices anyway.

On the other end of the spectrum, are solids companies that have been in their industries for a long time and are industry leaders. However, they don't have many followers in the stock market, and so their stock tends to track sideways. They're not very sexy.

Warren Buffet couldn't care less about sexiness. Instead, all he cares about is whether the company has solid fundamentals that will continue to produce solid results way into the future. He buys to own; he doesn't buy to trade.

The big disadvantage to this approach, however, is fundamental stocks have shown lackluster returns compared to high-flying stocks. Put simply, which stock would you rather get? A stock that doubles in price after five years or a stock that quadruples in three years?

Not surprisingly, fundamental stock trading, while it gets a lot of lip service from experts, isn't as sexy as growth trading. Many investors would rather pin their hopes on a company that is going to zoom up like a rocket because of market popularity and trends.

Technical Trading

Technical trading takes a completely different approach from fundamental investing. There's a big difference between trading and investing.

When you're doing fundamental analysis, you are investing. Why? You're buying into the future performance of the company because you trust its leadership, its growth potential, and believe in the company. You're all about the fundamentals that the company brings to the table.

Technical trading, on the other hand, doesn't really care about the company behind the underlying stock. I couldn't care less about whether the company is poised to dominate its industry and branch out into the future to generate tons of profit. That's not the issue. The issue with technical trading is the behavior of the stock of that company.

It's all about patterns. This form of stock trading pays attention to volume. It pays attention to closing and opening prices as well as day lows day highs. This approach uses heavy data analysis to find opportunities regarding stocks movement to take advantage of these for profit.

Moreover, technical trading focuses on short-term gains. In other words, you look at the stock's trends and choose to trade on a day-to-day or even hour-by-hour basis. You're just paying attention to how the stock price behaves so you could lock in on a pattern to earn gains for the day, week or month.

The big advantage of this approach is that you put less research on the nitty-gritty details of the company's value. You don't really look at the fundamental structure of the company, its cash flow or any of that. You're not paying attention to its balance sheet.

Instead, you focus on the statistical data of the stock price and the share volumes. You zero in on fast-moving data, and you make decisions accordingly. This offers a tremendous amount of benefits for people who are looking for a quick in-and-out way of making money off the stock market. You see the data trends. You make a bet and if that bet pans out, you lock in on a significant gain.

It's not uncommon for technical traders to set a limit of 2% per trade. It may seem like 2% is a small amount of money. But if you factor in the fact that these individuals trade hundreds of thousands, if not millions, of dollars' worth of stock with each trade multiple times in a given day, these small moves can translate to big money every single day.

The big disadvantage with technical trading is that there's a big divide between theory and practice. The theory that I've described earlier sounds exciting. I mean who wouldn't be excited about trading solely by numbers and the 'predictability' of patterns? You can see an indicator that a stock is trending up and, by all appearances, it looks like it's going to make you money.

However, in most cases, technical indicators are mixed. While some indicators might seem like the stock is going to do well in terms of its price movement, other indicators might send the opposite message.

You have to practice technical trading for an extended period of time so you can be as clear as possible as to these signals. This way, you will know when to enter a position and exit it. Otherwise, the information that you might get is so inaccurate that you end up essentially just gambling.

Another downside to technical training is the fact that oftentimes people who engage in this type of stock trading are going with the opinions of professional technical analysts. They let the analyst do the charting. They let the analyst come to the conclusion, and they're basically just placing their bets on such reports and analysis

This is a problem. If you're not doing your own charting, you are at the mercy of the technical analyst you're following. Understand that technical analysts just, like people in general, vary widely in their abilities. Some are really, really good; others are really, really bad. Unfortunately, even if you go with the really good technical analysts, they do have their bad days. If you follow them on a bad day, you may end up losing quite a bit of money. Technical trading is not a slam dunk, and you're essentially just betting all these thousands or hundreds of thousands of dollars on somebody's opinion.

Growth Stock Trading

Growth stock trading is a specialized type of trading where you invest in stocks that are appreciating faster than the general stock market. You look at past performance. You also look at their potential to go up in value even more.

The great thing about growth stocks is that you don't have to wait for them all that long. The majority of stocks that trade in the United States and elsewhere are actually trading sideways. You have to wait for them for quite some time for them to give you a decent return. This is quite attractive to a lot of people because it gives them some sort of calm, orderly assurance. These stocks are not volatile. They don't spike up and then crash back down.

However, if you're looking for solid returns year after year that can beat inflation by a factor of at least 5:1, look for more volatile stocks Look for stocks that can spike up and drift down and then spike up again. This is where growth stocks come in. Look for stocks that already have a track record of appreciating quickly. They should also have qualities may indicate that they would go up in value rapidly and substantially soon.

What should you look for when looking to trade growth stocks?

First of all, you need to set a budget. You have to have a maximum cap of around 30-40 price per earnings (P/E) per share. In other words, the stock price' is, at most, 40 times the per share earnings of the company. Buy in anywhere north of this and you're overpaying for the growth stock. Of course, the lower the PE, the more attractive that stock should be.

Moreover, please note that growth stock trading can also involve value trading or fundamental trading. Look at many different potential growth stocks and pick the ones with the most solid fundamentals. These are the ones who you think are most likely to break out in the future because they have stable foundations.

The big advantage with growth stock trading is that you get to ride high-flying stocks with a lot of market buzz and sizzle. This is a great and often quick way to increase your wealth.

The downside here is that it's too easy to focus on stock price growth and lose sight of ultimate value and fundamentals. Put simply, you may hang onto that stock for too long until the market wakes up from its hypnosis regarding that stock and falls out of love with it. Just as it shot up like a rocket, it can also quickly drop like a rock.

CHAPTER 4:

THE BASICS OF FUNDAMENTAL INVESTING

Fundamental investing really boils down to investing in a company because you believe in what the company is doing and its potential. This requires a lot more work than technical trading.

With technical trading, your data points basically begin and end with the performance of the stock. Now, your data set can extend for a long time in the past and can be projected quite some time in the future, but it only comes from one place. It only comes from the actual performance of the stock. There is no other source of data points. This gives you a greater sense of control.

With fundamental investing, you're focused on three key questions. Is the company making money? Will it continue to make money in the future? How well does it compare to others in its industry?

Now, it may seem that these questions are pretty simple and straightforward, but it really boils down to how you get information to answer these questions. Many analysts could try to answer these questions regarding a particular company and come up with completely different answers.

Fundamental investing, ultimately, is all about the midterm to long term value of the company. It's not really the stock itself that you're paying attention to, but the company's quality, how well it's doing, and how likely it is that it would do better in the future.

Another key aspect of fundamental investing is that you are looking for bargains. That's the bottom line. Either you are looking for a company that is underpriced by the market now or in the future.

It's easy to understand the first scenario. For example: Company A is doing really well in its industry. It is a market leader, has great products in its development pipeline, and possesses a tremendous client base. Still, it's in an industry that is, for some reason or other, not very sexy. Similarly, its growth rate is not as stunning as internet companies or other technology-based companies.

While this company is making more money than companies in sexier industries, it doesn't matter to the market. The market thinks that this company is simply just not interesting enough. However, when you look at the cash flow of the company, how much debt it has, and all other important factors, you can see that there is a tremendous amount of discounting going on as far as its market valuation. There's a big disconnect between what its stock price should be based on its earnings and earnings potential and what the company currently trades at.

The analysis above estimates the hidden value of the company as it stands now. There is also another way to do fundamental investing: forecasting a company's future worth.

Warren Buffet and other legendary investors often work this way. They don't mind paying a premium for a company now because they are so confident that the company is going to perform even better in the future, that they're actually getting in at a discount. This is one aspect of fundamental investing that you should also pay attention to.

The Big Challenge in Fundamental Investing

Trying to find a discount now, as far as the actual value of the company as it exists now, is actually getting harder and harder. As more analysts and value investors flood the market, there is less and less of these 'undervalued' companies because the price per earnings ratio of these companies tends to get bid up.

Now, these fundamental stock plays are not going to be at the same level as growth stocks, but their prices do tend to get bid up. The better approach would be to disregard their high prices now because, based on your projections, you see this company being a bargain based on its future performance.

Fundamental Investing Goals

What are the goals of people who invest using a fundamental investing strategy? First of all, they buy stocks in companies with solid fundamentals that are either low priced now or can be justifiably bought now at a high price because of projected future growth.

It's still the same strategy. You're looking for some sort of "under appreciation." You're looking for some sort of discount. There has to be some sort of disconnect between what the company is truly worth and its price currently or its price in the future.

What are the Fundamentals of a Company?

The operative word in the phrase "fundamental investing," of course, is "fundamental." So what is so fundamental about "company fundamentals?"

First of all, you're going to use financial statements issued by the company. These are required by law from public companies. Officer of a public company are required to make public their financial statements.

As a fundamental investor, you're going to look through a company's quarterly and yearly filings. You would then get a clear idea of the company's quarterly and yearly revenue, its income, and its growth trend. You are also going to pay attention to its profit margin, as well as its debt load and return on equity.

What is Return on Equity?

Return on equity measures how much profit the company produces per dollar invested in the company. This highlights the fact that the company is able to turn whatever amount of money is invested in it and grow it by a certain rate. Now, the bigger the rate, the better.

How do we arrive at ROE or return on equity? Take the total amount of money invested in the company, and divide it by the amount of profit generated by the company. This is your ROE.

It determines whether the company seems like it's making money, but is actually burning through a lot of cash just to produce income, or it's an actual money generator. Because you know you are looking at a very attractive company when it takes a fairly low amount of cash and is able to multiply it. The more cash it generates from actual investment inputs, the better that company looks.

Pay Attention to the Company's Overall Ability to Produce Positive Cash Flow

Cash flow is one of the most important factors a fundamental investor looks at. In fact, Warren Buffet makes a big deal out of cash flow. If you determine that a company has a positive cash flow pretty much throughout the year, then you can be more confident in the company. You would know that this company does not suffer from structural or operational weaknesses that may put it at a serious disadvantage if certain conditions come to pass.

For example, if a company suffers certain cash flow bottlenecks consistently throughout the year, this may be due to the fact that most of its money is tied up in accounts receivables. As long as that money can be successfully billed from the companies and individuals who owe that money, then the company is going to be making money.

What if for some reason or other the company's industry suffers a downturn and institutional clients can't produce the cash? This is going to be a serious issue.

The good news is you can see this a mile away when you look at the cash flow figures of a company. You can see whether it has a wide base of customers. You can see whether it has a diverse range of customers across a few industries. You can also see whether there are structural limits to where its cash is coming from.

Make Earnings Estimates for the Future

Another aspect of fundamental investing is that you make earnings estimates for the future. You don't just look at what the company is doing right now. For all intents and purposes, chances are, the company's performance right now is already baked into its stock price. Instead, you're going to make an educated guess as to how well it would do in the future. Based on current earnings, you're going to project its earnings estimates into the future.

Of course, this is not as simple as it may seem. You can't just do a straightforward projection. For example, if a company grew by 5% in the past 10 quarters, it doesn't make sense for you to automatically assume that it's going to grow at that same rate. You have to factor in what's going on in the general economy, the health of the specific industry the company is in, the state of the competition, and the specific growth rate of the different parts of the company. In other words, the projection must be conditioned by other factors. Otherwise, you might just be fooling yourself into thinking that, since the company has grown steadily in the past, then this automatically means it will continue in the future.

Conditions do change. Often times, they change overnight. Don't automatically assume the same growth rate. Factor in realistic parameters.

Beware of Expert Earnings Estimates

If you think you might have a tough time making earnings estimates for a company you're thinking of investing in or a company that you have already invested in, wait until you look at the work of experts. There are many stock market experts and company analysts. In fact, there's too many of them.

The problem is, a lot of them are associated with or come from' prestigious' trading houses and investment banks that it's too easy to give too much weight to them. Many investors think that as long as the estimates are 'official' statements of well-respected investment banks, they should trust it automatically. You have to look through the numbers the 'experts' processed and see if you would come to the same conclusion.

The good news about these analyst reports is that they include all the numbers that they considered when coming to their conclusions. They open this information so anybody who has the time and attention to detail can check out those numbers for themselves. It is your job to see if the numbers reasonably support the conclusions of the analysts.

You have to do this yourself. At the very least, skim or scan through the materials. Don't just agree automatically.

Product Pipeline Considerations

Another key factor to consider when doing fundamental analysis is how broad the product pipeline of the company is. This is very important because there are many companies who are making a lot of money, but their product lines are mature. In other words, it's going to be a long time until a new crop of products replaces their top earners. This is a big issue for pharmaceutical companies and other industries where patents expire over time.

Pay attention to this issue because you might be stepping into a trap. You might be buying into a company that may be on its way to a long, painful decline. It may have started already. You think you're getting into this amazing multinational big brand pharmaceutical company, but it turns out that a lot of their blockbuster drugs are already turning generic or only have a few years left of patent protection.

Don't get caught by surprise. Make sure that the product pipeline of the company that you are thinking of buying is robust enough to sustain continued growth. In the case of pharmaceutical companies, be clear on their patent acquisition plans-if they can't come up with products on their own, they should have solid plans for buying smaller companies with promising patent applications or current products.

Balance Sheet Analysis

Balance sheet analysis really gets to the heart of the value of the company. Seriously. If there are any two pieces of official, legally mandated disclosures that you absolutely need to pay attention to as a fundamental investor, it's the balance sheet and cash flow analysis.

The balance sheet simply takes the company's liabilities and deducts it from the company's assets. What's left is shareholder equity or the net worth of the company. This gives you a big picture view of what this company is truly worth.

Management Analysis

Depending on how long you've been investing and how many manager profiles you've checked out, management analysis might be useful for you. Pay attention to how visionary the leadership is.

Please understand that in corporate America, corporate competence is assumed. In other words, a company's officers are presumed to already know how to do their jobs. The big issue is whether they have a good idea as to what to do. In other words, do they have vision? The bigger the company, the higher the chance that it's going to attract top notch operators. These are people who know how to do things.

The big question: are they being guided by top brass leadership to do the right things that would position the company for continued dominance in the future or position the company for even greater heights? How do you analyze this factor when selecting stocks?

First of all, pay attention to how visionary its leadership is. Look at their official 'vision' statements or other public 'vision' statements. Pay attention to the track record of the results the team produces. Take a look at whether the results tend to grow over time. Finally, pay attention to the CEO. How long has he or she been on the job?

If the CEO has been at the helm for a long time, then you should think about succession issues. Who is slated to replace the CEO? Again, apply the analysis above to the successors. How visionary are they? Do they have a track record of producing results?

Sales Analysis

It's also important to look at the overall sales of the company and see if it is growing on a quarter over quarter basis. Now, a few dips here and there are okay. However, the company should be growing and it should be growing at a robust pace. If not, chances are other companies would look more attractive by comparison.

Disclaimer: don't hang your hat on this. This is not the one answer that should make you buy a stock or skip it. However, it does lay the foundation as to whether the company has a future. If sales are growing at a healthy clip on a quarter by quarter basis, then, with everything else being equal, this is a company to pay attention to.

Operating Income vs. Actual Income

Another way fundamental investors dissect companies is to pay attention to their operating income and compare it to their actual income. Income analysis is extremely important. The good news is, by law, the securities and exchange commission in the United States, requires public companies to release income statements. This is called 10K and 10Q filings. Pay close attention to these documents.

These documents are presented in a fairly clear way. You just need to look at certain lines in the report. First of all, you need to look at the net income line. This will tell you the profit the company earned... This is net income.

Sounds pretty straightforward, right? Well, not quite. You have to pay attention to non-recurring income or extraordinary charges.

For example, it may seem that a company lost money for the quarter. It may even be a very big loss. But if the report states that it is a one-time charge because the company's laying off people or shutting down divisions, you need to look closer. Why? When you discount these extraordinary items, it may well turn out that the company is actually making money.

Similarly, if the company made a tremendous amount of money in the past quarter, take a look as to whether this is non-recurring income or an extraordinary windfall. Sometimes, companies get a huge infusion of cash because they sold off a division or they sold off some assets. This may seem exciting because the net income blew up, but when you discount those, it may well turn out that the company is bleeding money and not doing really well.

In order for you not to get thrown off by the net income line, you should focus instead on reading income statements with an eye towards operating income. This is actual income from normal operations.

By normal operations, we're not talking about selling a division of the company or selling assets or any one-time situation. We're also not talking about adjusting tax brackets, which can only be done infrequently. Instead, we're talking about normal income generating operations. This is how well the company usually does on a day to day basis.

One key shortcut to determining operating income is to pay attention to a reporting line that says "earnings before interest, taxes depreciation and amortization" or EBITDA. This should give you a clear idea of the operating income of the company you are analyzing.

Cash Flow Analysis

In addition to income analysis, cash flow analysis is one of the most important analyses you could do if you are pursuing a fundamental investing strategy. With cash flow analysis, you pay attention to net income versus cash flow.

Net income really boils down to total profit. Revenues minus costs. This is a problem because sometimes, it can hide expenses, depreciation or credit costs. Cash flow, on the other hand, makes it much harder to hide these things. It also makes it harder to hide structural weaknesses in the company.

With cash flow analysis, you get to measure temporary losses that fund all the operations. You get a clear idea of a company's obligations and debts as well as the promotions it does. This analysis gives you such a clear view of a company's prospects that you should look for companies that have enough cash to cover all debt. It should have enough resources to take care of all marketing and operations and have cash left over for additional future projects.

If you look at the cash flow statement of a company and it shows that the firm experiences negative cash flow (at least two times per year), this should be a red flag to you. This highlights the fact that the company might be suffering from structural issues. It still makes a profit overall, but this provides cold comfort because there are certain rough patches the company goes through every single year. If you don't see this and business conditions change, it doesn't take long for that negative cash flow to translate into a loss for the year.

Where does negative cash flow stem from? It can be due to a small customer base restricted to a narrow range of industries or is restricted to just one industry. It can also arise when only one customer accounts for almost all the sales of the company. Cash flow issues can reflect the fact that most of the products sold by the company are sold on credit. This is the accounts receivable scenario I described earlier. Finally, cash flow issues also tend to shed light on slow product development.

Be very suspicious and concerned if any of these are in play as revealed in the form of negative cash flow. This doesn't necessarily mean that you have to completely avoid the company or just give up on it. Instead, this should prompt you to dig deeper as to its fundamental value and see if there are any other points of attraction in the company.

Earnings Per Share Analysis

Take the total net income of the company and divide it by the total number of shares outstanding. This gives you an earnings per share figure. Now, the next step is to take the current price of the company's stock and divide it by the earnings per share. This gives you a price per earnings ratio.

Now, what do you do with this ratio? Well, it's all comparative. You look at other companies in the same industry as the company you're analyzing and make sure that they share the same fundamentals. You don't want to compare apples to oranges. You want to make sure that you're comparing pretty much similar companies who deal with the same fundamentals.

After you have lined up these companies, pay attention to their price/earnings ratio or P/E. This should highlight which companies are expensive, which companies are relative bargains, and what is the industry average P/E.

Once you have these figures, compare these numbers with the P/E of companies in the overall stock market. By doing all these comparisons, you should get a fairly clear idea as to whether a company is trading at a bargain or whether it's overbought or overvalued.

Cash Flow Per Share Analysis

Take total cash flow figures from the operations of the company and divide it by the shares outstanding. You then compare this figure with cash flow per share figures from other companies within the same industry. Again, this should give you a fairly clear picture of how that company stacks up to the competition in terms of investment potential.

Combine Cash Flow and P/E Analysis

The next step is to combine both the figures you get from your cash flow and P/E analysis to determine which stock is underpriced. Many stock experts say that cash flow analysis is the best way to value and compare stocks.

Once you reach this stage, you have all the data that you need to properly compare stocks. You can only tell if something is a bargain if you compare it to something else.

You have to line them up and see where the numbers fall. You can't just automatically assume that since the company reached a certain threshold that it is necessarily a good deal. Don't compare it with itself or compare it so some sort of abstract ideal. Compare it to other companies in its industry.

Look for strengths that a company has that others don't have. On the flip side, always look for weaknesses that it has that others don't have and cross reference these or support these with the financial numbers they are legally required to supply. Once you have everything together, you can then properly size up which companies are good deals and which ones are trading at a steep premium.

CHAPTER 5:

THE BASICS OF TECHNICAL TRADING

After you've read the chapter on fundamental investing, you probably thought that it takes quite a bit of work. You would be absolutely correct because when it comes to trading based on the fundamentals of a company, you really have to dig into the data. And we're talking about many different data sets you're paying attention to: the balance sheet of the company as well as its cash flow, its income statements, and so on and so forth. It seems like you have your finger stuck in so many pies.

It's not unusual for people looking to do some fundamental investing to feel that they are in over their heads. It's just too much data. In fact, it's too easy to conclude that people can suffer from data overload.

Well, the good news about the alternative to fundamental investing is that you have less data and less data sources to work with. In fact, the data set only comes from one place-the actual performance of the stock.

Keep in mind that there's a big difference between the actual performance of the company behind the stock and the performance of the stock issued by the company. The former involves fundamental investing, while the latter involves technical trading.

The great thing about technical trading is that you're only focusing on the stock's behavior. You factor in volumes, volatility, and the price a stock opens at, where it closes, and its high point and low point for the day. You then keep track of this historically and from this fairly limited data set, you can make decisions.

There's a lot to recommend technical trading because if you are going to have to process and analyze hundreds of companies just so you can get a shortlist of underappreciated stocks for fundamental investing, it's easy to burn out. Seriously. It's just too much information. With technical trading, you can use software to filter the different stocks that have certain trading parameters and qualities. It's all based on the same narrow set of data so you can make decisions faster.

What is the underlying assumption of technical trading? There is a guiding idea behind technical trading: history can be used to make predictions.

Now, both you and I know, just because a stock behaved a certain way in the past, it doesn't necessarily mean that it would continue to behave the same way in the future. This is a simple fallacy because you can't just project the patterns that happened in the past into the future.

With that said, this is precisely the underlying assumption behind technical trading. With everything else being equal, past performance and past patterns can set the tone and direction of how a company's stock trades.

This is obviously not perfect. In many cases, stocks can surprise us. You might think that you have a slam dunk on your hands and it turns out that the stock starts to tank or trades sideways for a long time. Still, given the fact that there are so many people using technical trading to make money off the stock market, something has to be said about this assumption. At some level or another, it works.

You have to factor in quite a bit of data points. You should pay attention to the historical patterns of the stock price and you cross reference that with volume. By putting these two factors together, you can then forecast the stock's behavior.

The problem with forecasts is that they are, ultimately, just opinions. You're more than entitled to your own opinion as I am to mine. And if our opinions differ, then so be it. It's just really a matter of which opinion you find more persuasive. Everybody's entitled to their own opinion because people can look at the same set of data and walk away with two totally different conclusions.

The Bottom Line with Technical Trading

The big point of distinction between technical trading and fundamental investing is that this is all about trading. In other words, you are buying and selling based on the stock price itself. Fundamental investing, on the other hand, is all about the intrinsic value of the company behind the stock. You are investing or buying into the company because you believe in the company irrespective of its stock's performance.

Technical trading is all about data. We pay attention to the market trends, we pay attention to the movement of a stock, and we make really short term predictions as to how the stock would behave at a certain time. By paying attention to patterns and trends, technical traders profit by figuring out when to buy in and when to cash out.

This might all seem too theoretical and speculative. Believe me, it's very hard to track numbers in your head, especially if you're trying to make sense of opening price, closing price, day high, day low, and volume. There seems to be so many data points going in many directions. Thankfully, you can use charting to fix this problem.

Technical trading is heavy on charting. You chart the opening and closing prices per day, week, month and year. You also chart volumes of share sales. You also chart the overall progression of the stock over an extended period of time.

Charting gives you some sort of visual representation of all these different data points that are pulled from the same place. By being clear on all these data points and seeing the pattern, we can make decisions as to forecasts and bet accordingly.

What's Included in a Chart?

In a typical stock chart, you should insist on the following: you should at least know the opening price of a stock for the day, its highest price for the day, as well as its lowest. You should also see the closing price for the day and there has to be an indicator of the total number of shares traded that day.

Seeing all this information depicted in a chart and seeing all this information charted over a long period of time should open your eyes to the patterns the stock follows.

For example, you may be tracking a stock that predictably dips in the beginning of each quarter and then rises, and it continues to rise once the quarterly earnings are released. It then dips again at a certain time of the quarter only to increase in value later on. Knowing this through charting, you would be able to know when to buy in. You would know when to sell short and cover your short sales.

What are You Looking for When You Look at a Chart?

Day traders, technical traders and others who are very heavy on periodic stock action look for patterns. They're looking for price trends that they feel would give the stock's behavior some measure of predictability.

Once they determine the pattern, they would then test that pattern by using small trades. If the trades pan out, they increase their trade until they're making quite a decent sum of money betting on these day to day short-term patterns.

When you look at a chart, you should pay attention for patterns. These can play out day to day. Some stocks are so predictable that they actually behave in a fairly regular way in the course of a day. This is tremendous news for a technical trader because they can wait for the stock to dip for the day and then unload it when they see the trading pattern for the day's high become more and more apparent.

Day traders love day to day patterns because they can make the same bets over and over again to get roughly similar results. Often times, they make many different trades in the course of a day. Knowing the patterns and knowing the predictable nature of the stock can go a long way in determining whether you make money or not.

You should also look for multi-day patterns. Sometimes, a stock plays out in a predictable trading pattern for up to a week. It takes a few days for the stock to behave a certain way. For example, it would go up, and it would dip, and then it would bounce up much higher. This can happen in the course of a day or it can take several days for this to play out. The bottom line? You're going to be aware of this because you're using charts.

Longer term traders like swing traders would often look at multi-day patterns. They would look at how a stock pans out week by week or every two weeks. It really all boils down to predictability because if stocks continue to follow certain patterns like clockwork, you would know when to buy in and when to cash out. Find where in the pattern you're in and adjust your trading accordingly.

For example, one of the most common patterns in technical trading is a cup dip. When you look at the chart, there is the lip of the cup and it dips down just to follow the shape of the side of a cup. However, once the big dip is over and it starts sloping back up, it starts to dip again to form the handle of the cup.

If you notice this pattern in the stock that you are following, you can make certain predictions. You can identify where you are in the shape of the cup, and then plan accordingly. Maybe you are at the bottom of the dip, so you can go in there and scoop up quite a bit of stock at a discount, and then time your exit, based on when the cup handle will appear.

Common Patterns for Technical Trading

Cup with Handle

As mentioned above, when you see a cup pattern, a stock dips over time, creating a U-shape. Then the price goes back up, and then dips again as earlier low price buyers cash out. These are people cashing out for profits because they bought at the bottom of the dip.

When the cup goes up, and then it dips down again because of people exiting the stock (they already made their money so they exit), this creates a small U called the handle of the cup. Be on the lookout for this because it is quite common.

Head and Shoulders Pattern

One of the easiest patterns for newbie technical traders to trade is called the head and shoulders pattern. It's fairly easy to spot. A left shoulder forms when a stock increases due to heavy volume buying. There's a lot of volume in the stock and the initial peak forms.

When this happens, however, and the rest of the market detects a nice run up in the price of the stock, the market catches up and sellers line up to unload shares. This, of course, causes the price to dip. You get that first mountain that appears on the left side. It picks up and then it dips.

But pay attention to volume. You know you're looking at a classic head and shoulders pattern when the volume of stock purchases in the beginning, when it went up in price, is higher than the volume of the stock when sellers unloaded the stock. In other words, there is a net positive demand for this stock. And that demand is worth something because that demand is going to have consequences in terms of the stock's short term performance.

There's a disconnect between the buyers and the sellers when the first shoulder appeared. So the stock goes up first, and then it dips down as sellers start unloading their stock. However, they can't go on dumping forever, and this is why the volume at this point is lower than at the beginning of the rally in a particular stock.

Once the sellers have finished selling, since there's more demand than supply, market volume picks up again. Pay attention to this. The volume in selling is going to be lower than the initial volume, but once the head of the head and shoulders pattern starts to appear, the market volume picks up quite a bit.

At this point, the head of the pattern is created. Then volumes decrease again and this triggers selling, and the price drops. This creates the second shoulder. Newbies can ride this pattern to a tremendous amount of profitability because it is so regular.

Breakout Patterns

Breakout patterns are all about determining the limits of a stock's movement. When a technical trading analyst says that a stock is facing resistance, it means that the stock can only move up to a certain point until it can't move any further. This blocks further upward movement of the price. This is the stock's resistance level. Generally, the stock is moving up until it hits that ceiling and it can't get past that.

The opposite is also true. When a stock is sliding, it can keep dropping until it reaches a point where it can't drop any further. This is called the support level. A breakout happens when either a stock punches through the upper limit resistance or it crashes through the floor set by the support level.

One general rule of thumb that a lot of technical traders stick to when it comes to breakout patterns is that the longer a stock stays within a range of resistance and support, the more intense its breakout performance will be when the breakout finally happens.

If a stock keeps bumping against a resistance level and it can't move higher, enough demand may pick up and this can lead to a nice surge past the resistance level. The opposite, of course, is also true. A stock may be dipping and testing the support level continuously. Eventually, the stock, if there's enough selling activity, may punch through the floor value of the stock.

Double Bottom

Another pattern that's quite predictable is the double bottom or W-figure. For example, a stock would dip 10%, then it would rise, then it would dip again, and then it would spike up. The key is to find stocks that do this consistently and get in at the right time to ride the stock up or down.

Also, keep in mind that this pattern might not play out within the day. When you look at the chart, it might not have a W-figure within the day. It may take several days for this to play out.

Long Term Trend Buy Forecasting

Although technical trading is all about buying stocks based on chart performance, there is an element of fundamental trading involved as well when it comes to paying attention to long term trends. While you're still not looking at the underlying company's intrinsic value, you're looking at its overall long term stock performance value as revealed by its trend line.

You look at a multi-year chart of a company's stock prices. You then draw a line at the bottom of the lowest point and keep it below all the prices to the current day's prices. When you draw that line at the bottom of all the prices over an extended period of time, you would see that this creates a floor trend. Either the trend line is rising or it's sinking. You track this over the years. And even after factoring in breakouts and falls in stock prices, a clear trend line should still emerge.

Wedges

Another pattern to look at when doing technical trading involves wedges. You draw a top line trend. This is a line that's above all the highest selling price of a stock and draws it all the way to today. At the bottom, you should also do the same thing, but you trace the lower end of the stock's performance to today.

When you draw these two trend lines, you would notice that the highest pricing of a stock and its trend and the trend tracking the lowest pricing of the stock can meet in a triangle. This wedge-like triangle, also called flags, can have many different appearances.

It can be pointing up. This means that there is a stronger down trend in the stock and this indicates that, with everything else being equal, there's a good chance that that stock will sink in value. The flag can also be pointing down. This means it is facing heavier selling pressure and this can indicate that the stock might be gaining in value in the future.

It really all boils down to how many of these flags you see. If you see a lot more bullish signs, this could indicate a future rally. However, if you see more bearish flags, this can indicate a potential future collapse of the stock.

Pay close attention to these wedges because they can help you identify stock falls or stock rises. Use this information to buy in at the right time to lock in pretty decent profits.

Candlestick Chart

There are two ways to chart financial information. You can chart using bars or lines. A candlestick chart basically combines both a line chart and a bar chart. It tracks price and the movement of the price within a day in a single bar.

Now, when you put all these bars together, you can then see the general pattern in this stock's movement-especially when you see the highest and lowest price for the day.
What makes the candlestick chart approach interesting is that it can be color coded. You can create green or red charts. Green means that the stock finished in positive territory for the day. Red indicates the stock dipped for the day.

The candlestick chart is very, very useful. A lot of people prefer it over any other type of charting for doing technical trading because you are able to track the open and the close of the stock price for the day, and you also get all this information in one easy-to-spot graphic.

The Big Concept: Moving Average

If you want to get a big picture as to what a particular stock's prospects are, pay attention to its moving average. This is a number calculated using closing prices averaged over a period of time. This gives you a running idea of whether a price is cheap or expensive at any given time within a period because the moving average sets the parameters for the stock price. The average gives you a frame of reference for the stock's price at any given time.

Keep all the concepts above in mind when doing technical trading. This type of trading can be a lot of fun because the main thing that you're doing is you're just looking for patterns.

CHAPTER 6:
IDENTIFYING AND PICKING THE RIGHT GROWTH STOCKS

To recap, growth stocks are stocks that may not necessarily have strong fundamentals. Regardless, the stock market, for better or worse, somehow fell in love with these stocks. If you need a great example of a growth stock, take a look at Facebook or Tesla. Compared to other companies with stronger fundamentals, it's usually a no-brainer comparing the stocks of these high flying and heavily hyped companies with more solid companies.

In normal times, people would pick stocks that have zero to no debt, solid sales growth, industry domination and solid management as well as tremendous cash flow. Unfortunately, or fortunately, depending on your perspective, the stock market values stock primarily in terms of perceived growth potential. This is how stocks like Twitter were able to achieve some traction early on before gravity pulled them back down to earth.

One big danger with growth stocks is that, eventually, the stock market may fall out of love with you. That's the bottom line. When that happens, reality hits. It's as if scales fall out of people's eyes and they notice the huge amount of debt the company has. They start noticing that the company only has two or three major customers. They realize the company's cash flow over a four quarter period actually goes through some tremendous turbulence.

Unfortunately, if you're one of those investors who realize this later on after the stock has tanked, you're pretty much a day late and a buck short. Keep this in mind when it comes to growth stocks.

I don't mean to discourage you but we need to be clear as to what exactly we're looking at. These are not, generally speaking, fundamentally strong stocks.

With that said, one of the techniques that I will teach in this chapter involves using fundamental analysis to pretty much separate growth stocks in terms of likely winners and probable losers. Before we begin, let's do a quick recap.

What are Growth Stocks?

Growth stocks are shares of companies that appreciate faster and higher than general market indices like the Dow Jones Industrial Average index.

For example, the Dow Jones Industrial Average appreciates 20% year after year, you can bet that growth stocks leave that in the dust. We're talking maybe doubling in a year or possibly doing much better. Whatever the case may be, there is a big black and white difference between general index performance and growth stock performance.

Also, when you pay attention to the other stocks in these growth companies' industries, they leave everybody behind.

It's as if they are the Cinderella story of their particular industry.

Again, Tesla Motors is a good example of this. Usually, when people think of the automotive industry in the United States, they think of companies like Ford, General Motors, and others. But Tesla shines in this industry. It's as if gravity doesn't work on that stock. It seems that the normal rules that hold back and drag down automotive stocks don't apply to Tesla. It's as if investors hold it to a different standard.

It's easy to see why, because the resume of its CEO, Elon Musk, is more reminiscent of Silicon Valley and its high flying tech stocks than Detroit and the old industrial America that pretty much characterizes the US automotive industry.

Also, when you look at the specific underlying technology of Tesla, you really can't say that it is purely an automotive company. If anything, it's an electric motor vehicle organization.

With that said, Tesla is a growth stock because its rate of appreciation sets it apart and puts it head and shoulders above its competitors, both in its industry as well as in terms of the general industrial average. Keep this in mind when determining which stock, on its face, is a growth stock and which stock isn't.

Invest in Growth Stocks to Grow Your Wealth

What good are growth stocks for? If you are faced with two opportunities: investing in a solid company that dominates in its industry, has solid cash flow and is never in the red, or a company that just got started and admittedly gets a lot of media hype and love, which should you choose?

Well, it really boils down to what your objectives are. If you are looking for long term growth because you are investing your retirement money, chances are, you should go with solid companies with solid fundamentals. These are companies that are not going anywhere any time soon.

On the other hand, if you're younger or you just graduated from college and got your first corporate job, your objectives and mindset might be different. You might be in a hurry to grow whatever you managed to save in your 401K or IRA plan. If so, you might want to take a long, hard look at growth stocks because they are great for quick portfolio growth.

How much growth? We're talking about out-pacing the general market indices. Whether you're comparing your stock's growth to the S&P 500, the Nasdaq or the Dow Jones Industrial Average, you can bet that if you pick the right companies, you can get solid returns.

Before you get too excited...

It's easy to understand the concept of growth stocks, but picking out the right stocks is another matter entirely. So how exactly do you tell which growth stock is worth investing your hard earned dollars on?

What makes this complicated is that it's often hard to spot brand new growth stocks. These are stocks that, for the longest time, were just plodding along. They're basically just another company in the crowd. Not that many people are paying attention to them. Maybe only a handful of analysts would track their stock. All of a sudden, they start getting a lot of love and attention from the rest of the stock market.

It's hard to get in on growth stocks right at the point of ignition. It's easy to get in when they've already appreciated quite a bit. For example, Apple Computers was pretty much on its deathbed at certain levels during the period when Gil Amelio was the CEO of that Cupertino, California-based computer giant. The interesting thing about the Amelio period was that only a few people remember it. It was a time where Apple stocks were basically on life support.

And one of the best things that Apple did at that time was to buy out Steve Jobs' company, Next. Apple wanted Next not because of its computers, which was sold through a very narrow education-based marketing channel, but because of its operating system.

It turned out to be the defining point in Apple Computer's corporate history because the second act of the Steve Jobs era brought the iPod, the iPhone, the iPad and key innovations that blew up Apple stock to the stratosphere. But you would not have seen that coming when you saw how Apple's stock performance was plodding along at the end of John Sculley and Gil Amelio's leadership periods.

This is a classic example of a growth stock. If you owned Apple stocks at its lowest point at that period, you'd be a very, very wealthy person today. Apple has just basically blown up ever since that point, thanks to the amazing growth made possible by the iPhone.

I tell the story of Apple because it's easy to relate with that story. We're talking about a real company with real products producing real changes. Make no mistake about it, for better or worse, the iPhone and the age of consistent Internet connection changed the world.

Indeed, it was a fulfillment of CEO Steve Jobs' challenge to John Sculley when he hired Sculley from Pepsi. He said, to paraphrase, "You can spend the rest of your life selling sugared water, or you can change the world." And sure enough, Apple Computers changed the world.

Now, it's easy to see how Apple would be a growth stock, but I've got some sobering news. The vast majority of growth stocks out there are not of the same caliber as Apple. A lot of them are simply creatures of hype or market reputation. Whatever the case may be, the dollars that you make when you buy these stocks low and you unload them for a high price is all too real. In other words, you make the same real dollars trading these stocks as if you had traded Apple stocks.

The key here is to buy the right stocks before the rest of the market recognizes that the stock that you're buying is actually a growth stock. This is how you position yourself to become wealthy. As the old saying goes, you make your money when you buy.

Usually, when people think about earning a profit, they think about making the money when they unload. That's wrong.

You make your money when you buy. In other words, you recognize value that is unnaturally low or isn't being fully recognized by the rest of the market. This is the same philosophy that animates Warren Buffet's investment strategy. It's all about looking at unrecognized or unappreciated value.

How do you go about picking the right growth stocks?

Step #1: Compare stock growth over the same time frame with a broad index

For example, you're trying to determine out of a basket of 100 stocks which of these would make for a growth stock. You look at their individual performance over a fixed period of time and find the broad index growth rate. Whether we're talking about the S&P 500 or the Nasdaq or Dow Jones Industrial Average, it doesn't really matter. You would see which of these in a basket of 100 stocks grow at a very decent rate compared to the index.

Step #2: Compare stock growth over the same time frame to their industry's average

Now that you have filtered your initial basket of stocks, the next step is to look for their industry's indexes and compare their stock's growth over the same time frame. Again, after this step, you should be able to filter out some stocks from your list.

Step #3: Consistent stock growth over a significant time frame

What constitutes a significant time frame? Usually, 3-5 years is a good comparative time frame. Don't get too crazy with extending this too far back because the company, 5 years ago, might be a fundamentally different company and it would not make much sense to compare the company now to what it was before.

Maybe it was in a different industry, maybe it was run by a different CEO, maybe it had a different philosophy. Whatever the case may be, 5 years is a good enough time frame. Extending it way past that period might be counterproductive.

The key here is just to find some sort of consistency. We're talking about quarter over quarter growth, both in sales, earnings and stock price.

Step #4: Filter by P/E

Now that you have a fairly short list, the next step is to filter your list based on price per earnings ratio. A price per earnings ratio, as I explained earlier chapter, divides a company's current stock price by the amount of earnings per share the company has.

For example, if a stock is making $10 per share of profit and its current stock price is $200, its P/E is 20. Now, what is the upward limit of your P/E filter? 40 is a good cap. If you find a stock that is beyond 40, you might want to skip it.

Usually, the lower the P/E, the more attractive the stock. Anything under 40 means that there is still a way to go for the stock to appreciate. If you are looking at a stock that is already at 40 or close to 40, it's pretty much maxed out. Unless, of course, its earnings continue to grow at a healthy clip. This earnings growth could justify a higher stock price.

Step #5: **Compare growth stock candidates among the percentage of institutional owners**

This filter requires you to get to the nitty gritty of the company's SEC filings. The US Securities and Exchange Commission requires public companies to make a public filing of their percentage of institutional owners. In other words, how much of all their stock holders are pension funds, mutual funds, investment banks and other professional institutional shareholders. At this point, you're going to try to filter based on percentage of ownership. The higher the percentage, the better.

The reason for this is actually quite simple. When an institution buys millions of stocks in a company, it usually locks in a fairly long period of time-especially if they get a decent return. In other words, they don't freak out like an individual investor and liquidate their positions just because the stock experiences hiccups

Usually, they would stay for quite some time due to bureaucratic and institutional reasons. This provides quite a bit of stability. At the same time, this also makes the stock more attractive to other institutional owners because, usually, institutions tend to behave with a herd mentality. If they see that a lot of "smart money" is investing in one particular company, a lot of them would also want invest. But since they hold billions of dollars in assets, you can see that they can move quite a bit of stock and this can lead to some serious appreciation due to the volume involved.

Step #6: Consistent sales growth

Pay attention to a potential growth stock's financial filings. Look at whether its underlying sales are actually growing year over year. Usually, 10% appreciation is a nice benchmark. The more the better. What's important is its consistency.

In other words, it's okay if a company isn't appreciating 10% or more year after year in sales growth, as long as it is marching forward. In other words, in one year, it's 10%, and then it's 11% and 12% and so on and so forth. There can be dips, but as long as it's over a 10% threshold, this is a good sign.

Steer clear of companies that have flat sales or sinking sales. This can indicate a lot of things. Either they only have a small number yet high volume customers, or their industry is changing. It may well turn out that it's only hype or reputation keeping the company's stock up.

Don't be the investor who is left holding the bag when you bought in on hype and it turns out that the company's sales have been haemorrhaging for the past few years. Again, when doing sales growth analysis, keep it within a time frame that's manageable like 3-5 years.

Step #7: Track earnings growth

Look at the sales growth at Step #6 and pay attention to the total earnings of the company. Does it keep up with sales growth? Does it have a decent tracking with sales growth or does the company's earnings and sales go on opposite directions?

Step #8: Decreasing or low debt

Pay attention to how much debt a company has. Again, by law, American public companies release this information, so you should look into the financial statements of the company and look for its debt load. In particular, pay attention to its year over year debt level. Is it decreasing or does it maintain a fairly low amount of debt? On the other hand, is its debt load swelling?

Extra Research

Just in case you haven't tired of the 8 Steps listed above and you still have a lot of spare time, here is some extra research that you should do in determining whether your initial basket of potential growth stocks yields some gems.

Is the company a market leader? Pay attention to its market and see whether it's in the top 3. Analyze its industry and try to figure out if the industry is growing or undergoing a massive sea change.

Keep in mind that, thanks to technology, a lot of industries have been disrupted. For example, the compact disc industry is fairly small compared to its former self. The same applies to all sorts of optical media like DVD discs. Pay attention to the state of the industry. Is it undergoing disruption or is it growing?

Also, pay attention to the branding of the stock. As I've mentioned earlier, oftentimes, what separates a high flying stock from what would otherwise be a solid company that doesn't trade all that well is the amount of media mentions it has and how much the rest of the market has fallen in love with that stock. Pay attention to its brand. Does it have a solid brand? Is there massive market buzz?

Usually, when you detect this, this is reflected in the stock's price already. However, if you notice that there's not much market buzz around the company's products or it has few media mentions, you might have a gem in your hands if it has solid brands and a low stock price. You might be looking at an undiscovered or fairly obscure growth stock that may have a breakout point in the future.

Next, pay attention to its product line. Does the company have new products in the pipeline? How important are patents in the company's industry? Are we talking about a company that basically has mature product lines that may even go off patent? Pharmaceutical giants are the first ones that come to mind when it comes to this type of analysis.

Finally, does the company look like it's poised for market domination? Does it have a certain sub-niche that we can reasonably say it's either poised to take over or it has already taken over but the market hasn't caught on yet?

Again, with all these filters that I've given you, you should have more than enough to go with in terms of figuring out which company it might be on the brink of a nice stock breakout. Breakouts happen when the rest of the stock market starts paying attention to a company because the market finally wakes up to the tremendous amount of value the company brings to the table.

The next step, of course, is to buy in and hold growth stocks for short term to mid-term gain. The key to growth stocks is you should not hold them forever unless they have become blue chip stocks or they have really solidified their position that they make for great fundamental long term plays.

Remember to Switch From Growth Stock to Growth Stock

Keep in mind that what makes a growth stock a growth stock is the fact that there's a tremendous amount of market buzz around it. Please understand that the party is not going to last forever. The love affair is probably going to be short lived. Do yourself a big favor and be ready to switch from growth stock to growth stock.

You're chasing after return on investment. You're chasing after appreciation. You're not necessarily falling in love and getting married to the stock. It's not a long term commitment. Be ready to hit the exit button.

The bottom line with growth stock is actually quite simple. You're just trying to hitch a ride on different stock's growth rate. If done right, don't be surprised if your portfolio appreciates by double digits or even triple digits year after year.

CHAPTER 7:
IDENTIFYING AND PICKING THE RIGHT INCOME STOCKS

How would you like to buy a stock that not only goes up in value over time, but also pays you money for owning it? That's right, it pays you a dividend. Sounds awesome, right? Well, there's actually a lot more to the picture.

While income stocks do have a lot going for them, you have to play them right. You might end up buying an asset that doesn't compare all that favorably with other stocks. While you're still making money with that income stock, you might be missing out on better portfolio growth rate because you didn't invest on other stocks like growth stocks.

Keep in mind that when it comes to stock investing, you have to pay attention to two factors: return on investment and opportunity costs. If you invest in income stocks, you can get a nice ROI, but the problem is, your ROI or return on investment is not free floating. It only makes sense when you compare it with other investments.

For example, your income stock appreciates 8% per year and gives you some dividends, but your portfolio could have appreciated 25% if you invested in growth stocks. Technically speaking, as far as your opportunity costs are concerned, you're in the hole at least 17%. See the problem?

Before we get into any further details about income stocks, let's do a quick recap.

Definition of Income Stocks

When you invest in income stocks, you're investing in stocks that pay a dividend. A dividend is the share of the profits the corporation evenly splits among all its shareholders. For each share of stock a shareholder has in the company, they get a dividend distribution.

Now, keep in mind that this is not free money because you're going to be taxed on it. Also, it is your "compensation" for owning a company that made a profit. This money is hard won by the company you own.

This might seem pretty straightforward, but actually it isn't because you have to pay close attention to how much money you spent to get the right to collect the dividend. This is how you determine the yield that you're getting from your income stocks.

To do this, you need to measure the payout by dividing the dividend by the stock price. Put simply, you divide the amount of money you're getting from the company based on how much you paid to buy into the company to qualify for the dividend in the first place.

Who Should Buy Income Stocks?

As mentioned earlier, different groups of investors have different strategies. It really all depends on their objectives.

When it comes to income stocks, it's easy to see that they provide some level of security and assurance. Not only do you stand to benefit from the increasing value of the stock, but you also benefit from the dividends being issued by the company.

Not surprisingly, conservative investors tend to buy income stocks. There's a measure of assurance from the income while they're waiting for the stock price to go up over a fairly long period of time. In other words, they win twice. They get a current cash flow while the underlying asset goes up in value over time.

Short term income seekers also benefit from income stocks because even though they're not interested in long term stock growth, they get an immediate income from the stock. Many of these would buy the stock before the effective date of the dividend so they can lock in on the dividend, and then they unload the stock when it appreciated from the point they got in.

In other words, even though they're not making a tremendous amount of money from the appreciation of the stock, they still come out ahead because they are entitled, legally, to the dividend issued by the company behind the stock for every share they own.

Finally, dividend reinvestment investors are excited about income stocks. They would buy only income stocks and any dividends produced by these stocks are then quickly used to purchase even more shares. Think of this as compounding interest. You get an asset that grows over time and you use the cash flow from that asset to buy even more of that asset.

How Much and When are Dividends Paid Out?

Now that I've gotten you excited about the concept of dividends, how do they work? How much do companies pay in dividends and when do they pay them out?

Well, please keep in mind that not all companies issue dividends. In fact, the companies that do are actually in the minority. A large chunk of companies traded on Wall Street don't issue dividends. The ones that do vary tremendously.

It really all boils down to their earnings for the year and the discretion of the board of directors. Some companies issue dividends like clockwork. Every year the dividend must come out. Some companies skip a few years and then they issue a dividend then they skip a few more years, and so on and so forth.

When companies do decide to issue a dividend, it's usually paid out quarterly. The amount of cash that you get at the end of every quarter is one fourth of the annual dividend figure.

How do you qualify for the dividend? When do you need to buy the income stock so you can get your hands on the dividend?

Well, dividends are paid out to stockholders of record before the 'strike date.' The company would announce the strike dates so if you buy the stock before this date, you qualify for the dividend. As mentioned above, dividends don't always occur year after year. By the same token, they can also fluctuate in value year after year.

Some companies are steadier when it comes to dividend payouts. For example, utility companies like power companies or water companies in the United States tend to be very predictable as to how much money they would pay out every year, as well as the consistency of the payouts.

Please note that, from time to time, dividends can be cut off completely. Remember, dividends are products of the corporation's board of directors' discretion. So if they decide that the company is going through tough times or the company needs cash for capital expenditures to build out a division or to go into a new direction, they can cut off the dividends.

The good news, however, is that most don't because they know that a lot of investors buy into their company just for the dividends. They also know that a lot of people are depending on the dividend. Their stock value would probably take a big hit if they cut off dividends.

Finally, please note that dividends usually increase to beat inflation. It's fairly rare where you see a company that sticks to the same low dividend for 50 years straight. Usually, the dividends increase at some level to beat inflation.

Why Should YOU Buy Income Stocks?

First of all, income stocks are great as defensive purchases. They help you defend against inflation. Also, there is a ready demand for this type of stock because, like you, other investors are afraid of inflation.

Also, when there is pressure on the stock price of the dividend issuing company, the fact that it issues dividends shields the stock somewhat during a sell off.

Next, income stocks are often viewed as "safe stocks" or even "defensive stocks." These are stocks of companies that offer goods or services that are still demanded even in economic downturns. As I have mentioned earlier, a lot of the dividend-paying companies in the United States are utilities like water, gas, and energy companies.

Please note that income stocks tend to be industry clustered. Certain industries tend to have companies that are more likely to issue dividends than other industries. These include, but are not limited to, utilities, as mentioned earlier, REITs or real estate investment trusts, and energy stocks. Sounds awesome, right? Sounds like a walk in the park?

Not quite. Why? Dividend-issuing companies are very sensitive to interest rate changes. A dividend's return is measured in percentage points. If the percent you get off your dividend is lower compared to certificates of deposits, treasury notes or other investments, income stock holders often dump their shares. This is not a terribly bad thing for new buyers because this can improve the yield of the stock and the stock can go back on an upswing.

Please note that although most companies raise their dividends to beat inflation, not all do. When you're doing your due diligence looking for income stocks to buy, pay attention to how often the company raises dividends and whether this is enough to make headway against inflation.

How to Buy Income Stocks

Now that I have gotten you excited about income stocks, the next step is to figure out how to buy them. First, you need to figure out how much cash you need every year. This is the income that you are going to try to generate from your stock holdings or your bond investments.

The next thing that you need to consider is how much in taxes you're going to pay. Always factor in taxes. As the old saying goes, there are only two things that are certain in life: death and taxes. Come up with a tax-adjusted income figure. This is the figure that you're going to be earning from your stock holdings.

Next, figure out how much cash or existing investments you need to produce tax adjusted income. In other words, how much cash do you need to come up with to buy a stock to produce a tax adjusted income? This is your income stock capital. After doing this analysis, you should determine your target rate of return.

All the other analysis that I've listed above should spell out what your target rate of return should be. Next, hunt for stocks that meet your percentage rate of return. Sounds simple, right? However, there's a question that most intermediate investors ask: Why not just buy bonds that pay a certain rate?

The answer? Inflation. If inflation is 0%, you can do percentage rate bonds. But if you buy income stocks, the stock growth plus the periodic increases in dividends effectively neutralizes inflation. Not so with fixed rate bonds.

Always factor in inflation. It's easy to think that if you need 8% per year on your money so it would continue to grow and you would continue to live without having to work, don't be surprised if inflation rears its ugly head and bursts your bubble. You can't just automatically assume that if you need 8%, you just need to get 8% corporate bonds. It doesn't work that way.

Buy Income Stocks Based on Yield

Yield is a crucial distinguishing point for income stocks. Yield is calculated by dividing dividend income by the stock's price. In other words, you divide the amount of money you're getting from the stock by the amount of money you spent to buy the stock in the first place. The higher the yield, the better. However, yield is tricky because it depends on the changing price of the issuing stock. Yields change depending on the stock's overall performance.

Keep all these in mind when looking for income stocks. They are definitely nifty and can help you with your financial planning goals, but you need to know what you're doing, otherwise, you may be stuck with a loss in terms of opportunity costs.

CHAPTER 8:

PICKING AN INVESTING STRATEGY THAT SUITS YOU

At this point, you should be clear as to how fundamental investing works, how technical trading operates, and how to pick growth stocks. You also should have a fairly clear idea of how to pick an income stock. Now, with all that knowledge out of the way, we need to focus on a fundamental question.

You already know that you want to do something with that pile of dollars you worked so hard for. Currently, it's in the bank, and you and I know, that that is the worst place for your money. In fact, it's only a step away from stuffing your money into mattresses. The end result is actually the same because banks pay so little interest that inflation, sooner or later, would eat up the purchasing power of your saved dollars.

You need to do something with that money. You should, at this point, be clear as to what your objectives are. Are you trying to protect the value of your money because you're about to retire? Are you trying to grow your money because you're a fairly young person and would like to multiply your cash? Maybe you'd like a nice mix of both? Perhaps you'd like to generate an income from your money? You should have a fairly clear answer at this point.

In this chapter, I'm going to walk you through key selection factors regarding strategies. You have to be as clear about these as possible. They have to make sense as far as your personal set of circumstances is concerned.

You shouldn't invest in stocks a certain way or adopt some sort of strategy just because people you respect and admire do the same. Their particular set of circumstances might be different from yours. Their needs and preferences might be different from yours. You have to adopt a strategy that makes sense to you personally. It has to suit you because this is your money we're talking about.

Assuming You'll Be Picking Your Own Stocks

At this point, we're going to assume that you're going to be picking your own stocks and you're not going to put your money in mutual funds so a professional fund investor will take care of your money for you.

We're assuming that you're not using a professional investment vehicle outside of a mutual fund because, again, in that situation, somebody else is going to be doing the hard calls for you. Instead, we're going to be assuming that you, yourself, will be the only person that would select the stocks that you are going to buy to either protect the value of your money, grow your money, or generate an income, and anything in between.

Assuming that you're going to take ownership of this project, you have to answer the following questions.

How Much Time Do You Have?

How much time do you really have for investing? Keep in mind that investing doesn't just mean picking a stock, buying, and selling. There's a lot that has to happen for you to do that well. You have to buy analysts' reports, you have to read these reports, you have to get all sorts of data, you have to research. You need all this information so you can make a truly informed decision.

In many cases, a lot of these materials are not free. Sure, there are lots of blogs, websites, social media pages that give you all sorts of analysis, but if you really want the good stuff, you would have to pay for it because chances are, the stuff that's publicly available on Bloomberg, CNBC, and similar sites is stuff that other investors have beat to death. In other words, there's really not much movement there if you're looking for solid value.

For example, if you're looking for a growth stock that is a gem that other stock market players haven't fully recognized, it probably would be a good idea to spend a tremendous amount of your own personal time finding such a stock. Otherwise, get comfortable with ponying up a decent chunk of dollars for professional analysts to isolate these companies for you.

What Percentage of Your Investment Portfolio Can You Stand to Lose?

I don't mean to throw water on your plans to grow your money, but we're talking about stocks here. Stocks can go up-

and they can also go down. Now with all that said, even if a stock crashes, it doesn't necessarily mean that you lost money.

This is what we call a paper loss. It's only a loss in terms of the actual market value of that stock if you were to decide to sell it today. But assuming that you're not going to be selling, it's just a loss on paper. Things may well turn around and you may have a paper profit on your hands in no time.

With that said, there are certain situations where you feel that you have to liquidate your position. You just have to exit the stock. If that's the case, what percentage of your investment portfolio can you stand to lose? Can you waste $25,000 or 25%? Can you stand to lose a million dollars or 10% of your portfolio?

It really depends on your income, what your other assets are, as well as your overall net worth, as well as the 'emotional value' of your funds. There is no right or wrong answer here. This is truly personal to you.

Some people who are worth billions may turn out to actually have a very low loss appetite. In other words, they can't stand to lose even a hundred thousand dollars. On the other hand, a person who may be worth a million dollars, might actually be okay with losing $500,000 if it means he or she can stand to gain another $2 million.

Again, loss appetite varies from person to person. It depends on how you were raised. It depends on your values and priorities. It also depends on your personality. It depends on your past experiences. It all boils down to risk appetite. And when it comes to this factor, there are really 3 kinds of investors.

Aggressive investors

These are proactive investors who are ready to lose 50% or more of their portfolio value in exchange for the hope that they could gain so much more. We're talking about doubling their money or tripling their money. They're okay with losing half or even all of their money.

Moderate Investors

These individuals believe in putting a cap to the amount of losses that they could potentially suffer from the stock market. This, again, varies from person to person. But usually, a moderate investor tries to cap his or her losses at 33% or lower.

Conservative investors

These are people who either cannot stand too much risk or they're close to retirement. In the latter case, they know that their income will come from fixed sources and they won't be making as much money as before, so they basically have to live on a fairly predictable rate of return.

Conservative investors really cannot mess around with the stock market all that much. As I mentioned earlier, at best, only 20% of your total investment portfolio should be in stocks and those stocks must almost all be blue chips or tried and proven stocks that appear that they won't be going anywhere any time soon.

How Patient are You?

This is a very important question that a lot of other investment books do not ask. I need you to give me a straight answer because you have to be clear as to how patient you really are. A lot of people try to invest in the stock market in a very conservative way. They only invest maybe 20% of their investment portfolio and they try to play really safe stocks.

So far, so good, right? Well, the problem is, they're also very impatient. They have the mindset of people investing in growth stocks while at the same time investing almost purely in conservative stocks. Do you see the disconnect? What's wrong with this picture? So you have to factor in how patient you are.

If you are the type of person who can patiently watch grass grow, chances are, a conservative investing strategy would work out well for you. Even if a stock trades sideways for a long period of time and goes quarter after quarter of almost no visible breakouts, then you'll be okay.

On the other hand, if you're not a very patient person, then you either have to invest in mutual funds so somebody else would do the waiting for you, or you might want to switch your investing strategy to something that fits your temperament.

How Old are You?

Your age, believe or not, plays a very big factor in how you should invest. If you're below 40, knock yourself out with growth stocks. You can afford an aggressive investment strategy if you're in this age range.

If you are 40-50 years old, you should start looking at more moderate investment strategies because it's only a matter of time until retirement is around the corner. If you're over 50, you really have no choice but to play things conservatively.

While it's theoretically possible that your nest egg, when invested properly in the right growth stocks can double, triple or even quadruple, it's also just as likely that a huge chunk of your saved assets would go up in smoke. You don't want out in the worst way possible because you're only a hop, skip and a jump away from retirement.

Available Strategies

To recap, what are the stock trading strategies available to you? Again, your selection here depends on the questions I posed earlier.

Fundamental Investing

Fundamental investing is a very powerful and conservative approach to growing your money. The downside is that it requires a lot of time and resources and it turns on accurate data about the company. If you're going by hype, if you're going by reputation, then all bets are off.

Technical Trading

Technical trading requires software. You also need a fast trading platform. You can't be a slowpoke when doing technical trading because the window of opportunity that you're trying to lock into may have passed or disappeared the moment your trade is fulfilled.

You need a very fast trading platform. A lot of big time traders who do technical trading use lightning fast or almost instantaneous trading platforms.

Also, you need to invest quite a bit of your personal attention in technical trading. You basically have to watch the stock you're trading like a hawk so you can see opportunities, jump on them, lock in, and either register a loss or cash out at a profit and then look for the next opportunity.

Technical trading, believe it or not, requires a tremendous amount of discipline because it's easy to think that just because you traded well, that your luck will continue. This is what kills the profits of too many technical traders. They just let their position ride for too long. You should set clear return goals for yourself.

If your goal for the day is to secure a 5% return, the moment you achieve it, stop. Start again the next day. Similarly, if you are a longer term trader and your goal is to register 10% over a week or more, if you're able to hit that point, stop.

A lot of technical traders often end up reversing or undermining their initial gains because they just can't stop trading.

Growth Stocks

With growth stocks, you need to be able to look at current trends and spot hot stock clusters. Using the step by step analysis I mentioned in an earlier chapter, you should be able to filter this cluster of hot stocks to really focus on long term growth stocks as well as short term growth stocks. In fact, the more fundamental value there is on a heavily hyped stock, the higher the likelihood that you can ride it safely to higher and higher prices.

CHAPTER 9:
HOW TO RESEARCH STOCKS?

Researching stocks really boils down to whether you're going to do it by yourself using your own resources and your own time, or you're going to basically look for secondary information. Secondary information, of course, means analyst recommendations. These are people who release special reports to a select group of investors or they publish stuff in widely available media and the information is free.

Whatever the case may be, you yourself are not doing the initial research. Instead, you're just taking other analysts' recommendations and going with their opinion. Keep in mind that these are opinions. Just like any other opinion, they can be right or they can be wrong.

Solo Research

If you're going to be researching stocks by yourself, use industry lists. These are publicly traded companies sorted by industries. The reason why I recommend you start with such list is because it's fairly easy to compare one industry to another.

Certain industries are growing. Certain industries have very bright futures. Certain industries are actually mutating into a wide range of the sub-industries. There's a lot of money flowing through certain industries.

Other industries are not doing as well. They're either under a tremendous amount of technology disruption like automation, artificial intelligence or machine learning, or they are being folded into other industries. Pay attention to how well industries are doing and pick hot ones.

Once you have a clear idea as to which industries are growing and show a tremendous amount of promise, the next step is to get industry lists of publicly traded companies within those industries.

Using the steps mentioned in a previous chapter of this book, filter all these companies. Go company by company. Once you have isolated an industry, get the company listing for that industry and filter each company one by one.

Use cash flow analysis if you don't have much time. With everything else being equal, if you don't really have the time to do a thorough job using all the public filings of a company, use cash flow analysis. This is where you should start. You then use cash flow per share analysis as well as paying attention to the P/E ratio of the company.

If you have followed the fundamental analysis steps I've mentioned earlier, you definitely need a lot of time to really get to the bottom of the value of each of the companies on an industry list. In fact, you would take quite a bit of time filtering the list.

The good news here is that since you're doing it on your own, there's a good chance that you might uncover some gems. You might discover some companies that the stock market hasn't paid enough attention to yet. The company might be a sleeper or a Cinderella company.

Analyst Recommendations

If you don't have the time to do solo stock research, you could always go with analyst recommendations. There are two types of recommendations. There are recommendations that are sold only to a small list of subscribers. These are specialized newsletters and can cost quite a bit of money because the analyst put in the time, effort and energy that you could otherwise have put in yourself. In other words, they're doing your job for you. Since they've done that, they need to be compensated, and a lot of these newsletters can be quite pricey.

The big advantage of using analyst recommendations is that they are industry specialists, by and large. These analysts specialize in certain types of industries and they would release industry-specific analysis.

Also, they have a tremendous amount of resources at their disposal. They can access all sorts of databases. They have all the tools that they need to crunch the numbers and come up with solid picks that may have a higher chance of being accurate.

When you tap the expertise of these analysts, you are dealing with people who are experienced in picking stocks. This is what they do. This is what they were trained for. This is what they live for.

The big downside to going with analyst recommendations is, of course, cost. If you are buying specialist analyst newsletters and these people are not connected to any investment bank or financial institution, expect to pay through the nose because independent analyst recommendations can be quite expensive.

If you were to rely on an investment bank's analyst because they issue a public list of recommendations, this can also be problematic. Why? Public expert recommendations and lists that come out of them are probably priced out. In other words, people already bought into the stock after the recommendation. In fact, chances are, that expert is not the first person to recommend the stock.

Finally, if you were to rely on investment bank's research department's recommendations, there are conflict of interest issues. It's not uncommon for investment bank analysts to have a very favorable view of a stock partly because the company they work for has a vested interest in the stock. Keep this in mind.

CHAPTER 10:

POOLED INVESTMENTS: ARE THEY RIGHT FOR YOU?

After reading all the chapters in this book up to this point, you probably think that stock investing is a tall order for you. You might be thinking that since you have a lot of other things going on in your life and the fact that time is a luxury for you, you might not have what it takes to invest on your own. You might have arrived at the conclusion that the best way to invest would be to simply find professionals that would handle your investments.

It's easy to understand this perspective. It's easy to see why a lot of people, especially when they're just starting out, would prefer that their funds be professionally managed. After all, these individuals have been in the game for far longer than you. They know how things work like the back of their hands. A lot of them have a solid track record of producing success.

With that said, just because you have decided to hire a professional to handle your investment, this doesn't mean that you can just pick any mutual fund. This doesn't mean that you should just pick a random fund out of a hat. Just like with picking stocks, you need to size them up and compare them properly. This way, you increase the likelihood that you would be making a truly informed decision.

This is crucial because if you make decisions on a whim or through incomplete or even incorrect information, it's anybody's guess whether you would get the return that you are looking for. In fact, you run the risk of not getting a return at all.

It's one thing to realize that you may not have the time and the expertise at the present time to make your own stock pick so you get expert assistance. It's another matter entirely to just basically roll the dice.

Make sure that pooled investment is right for you and make sure that you pick the right choice as far as your options are concerned.

Mutual Funds

Mutual funds are the meat and potatoes of many small investors. A lot of individual investors love the fact that mutual funds are professionally managed by people who have many years of experience in the fund management industry.

These individuals know the ins and outs of the stock market. They have access to a tremendous amount of research resources. Chances are quite good that these individuals would at least produce a decent return as far as the Dow Jones Industrial Average is concerned.

The great thing about mutual funds is that you are relying on somebody else's expertise. They are headed by a professional manager. Individual investors like you buy into the fund. In a way, it's like buying stock, but instead of a stock in a company, you buy a stake in the mutual fund, which gives you a share of its total asset value per investment unit.

You're buying an investment unit and this unit goes up and down in value based on the underlying stock prices of its assets. A mutual fund, really, is just a basket of stocks in different proportions that the fund manager bought into. When you buy into a mutual fund, you get an investment unit at a certain price.

However, that price tends to go up or down, depending on how well the stocks that the mutual fund invested in do. If the fund manager does an amazing job of picking more winners than losers, the total net asset value goes up, so your investment unit is worth more.

Different Types of Mutual Funds

Keep in mind that mutual funds pretty much mimic the different investment strategies individual investors could pursue. There are income mutual funds that focus solely on dividend-paying stocks.

Other funds focus on growth. These growth funds actually are quite diverse. Don't let the name throw you off. It's easy to think that if a fund is a growth fund, then you are necessarily dealing with an aggressive investment strategy.

Not necessarily. Some growth funds are quite moderate. Their main focus is on solid, stable, predictable growth of companies with real potential, not just market hype. There are also index funds.

Index funds are essentially mutual funds that enable you to bet on how the market overall is trading. All it does is it just tracks a certain index. For example, if you buy a Dow Jones Industrial Average index fund, the contents of that mutual fund are the stocks that comprise the Dow Jones Industrial Average.

This is just one type of index fund. In fact, there are many different indexes out there. There are also metals indexes or commodities indexes. When you buy into these funds, they invest in a way that tracks those specific stocks, specific industries or specific commodities. This way, when you like the progression of a particular industry, you can bet on that industry as a whole through an index fund.

Advantages of Mutual Funds

I've already referred to these a bit earlier. The main reason why people go into mutual funds is that they are managed by people whose job it is to watch the stock market. Their job is to look for opportunities. Their job is to get into a stock at the right time and leave at the right time to maximize profits.

Unlike you, they devote all their time to making sure that the mutual fund is positioned to register a profit. These managers have the time that you don't. That's what you're paying them a premium for.

Also, mutual funds are diversified. They don't put all their eggs in one basket. When a mutual fund focuses on income stocks, you can bet that it buys many different income stocks from many different industries. This way, when certain industries go south or certain individual stocks experience bad times, the rest of the good picks will ensure a fairly even valuation for the mutual fund's portfolio.

Another great benefit of buying into mutual funds is that even if you have very little capital, you can still buy into a mutual fund that would, in turn, be able to buy expensive growth stocks. Individually, you might not be able to buy much of those growth stocks, but if you buy an investment unit in a mutual fund, the mutual fund would have enough aggregate or pooled capital to buy expensive growth stocks and benefit from the growth of those stocks.

This pooled capital buying ability should not be taken lightly. It gives your small amount of cash quite a huge amount of leverage. You joined a pool that would be able to buy larger blocks and this enables potentially larger profits.

You have to understand that the stock market has a multiplier effect. The more stocks you buy and the higher the stock price goes, the larger your gain. However, if you can only afford to buy a handful of stocks, even if the stock performs really well, your overall profits aren't that big. Compare this to a situation where you were able to buy a huge block and the stock performs halfway decently. Do you see how pooled buying works out?

Disadvantages of Mutual Funds

The first drawback is the fact that a fund's past performance is no guarantee of its future performance.

There are many mutual funds out there that have great years. Some perform way better than the average mutual fund. But this doesn't necessarily mean that you should just jump in with both feet and invest everything you have into that mutual fund. Maybe it had a nice 5-year or 3-year streak, and then this year, it's going to hit a wall. Believe it or not, mutual funds suffer from both winning and losing streaks.

The flip side is also true. Maybe the mutual fund has had a very turbulent past 5 years where it's just going up and down and it's all over the place. But it turns out that this year, it's going to go on a very even upward trajectory. You just never know.

There's only so much trust and weight you can put into past performance. You have to look at other factors. Plus, keep in mind that management fees can cut into the net asset value of a mutual fund.

Different mutual funds feature different fee structures. Pay close attention to the fees because you wouldn't want a lot of the profits that you would be making off your investment being leached out by really high management fees. Also, take note of how fund managers are compensated. Sometimes, mutual funds still pay managers even if the mutual fund did not make money or outperform a certain average.

The whole point of investing in a mutual fund is that you're betting that you would get a better return than if you had invested individually.

CONCLUSION

Congratulations for reaching the end of this book. You now have all the information you need to start investing. I encourage you to start investing now. Why? There is such a thing called the compounding effect. The longer you wait to invest, the less your money will appreciate.

This is why it's a good idea to start investing in a mutual fund or 401K when you're in your 20's. Thanks to compounding (where the growth of your portfolio is reinvested as well as supplemented by new investments), you end up with a bigger pile of money when you're 65.

Compare this with the situation where you started investing when you're in your 50's. When the time comes to retire, your nest egg isn't going to be as big. Take advantage of the time element.

Invest now. Don't wait until everything is "just right." Don't wait until it "feels right." No. Focus on the compounding effect and if you still get cold feet as far as investing on your own are concerned and making your own individual stock picks, you can always invest first in mutual funds.

Once you have found the time to learn more about the stock market and stock investing, you can then start making your own individual trades. Also, make it a point to invest consistently. Not only should you start now, but you should put in money automatically into your investments on a very consistent basis over the long haul.

This doesn't have to involve thousands upon thousands of dollars every single month. It can be something as basic as $200 stored away month after month, year after year, decade after decade. You can bet, thanks to the compounding effect and proper investment management, that pool of money will not only beat inflation, but can grow to a substantial size given enough time.

Invest today. You will thank yourself for it later.

We hope you enjoyed reading! Please share your story by leaving an **Amazon review**. Every review is meaningful for us- We read them All.

Best Regards,
David Morales

A FREE BOOK TO OUR READERS

DON'T DIE BROKE

10 Key Facts That Ensure Financial Comfort

Download Here:

https://investingmoneymastery.com/ddb

NEXT READ

STOCK MARKET INVESTING FOR BEGINNERS

Simple Stock Investing Guide To Become An
Intelligent Investor And Make Money In Stocks

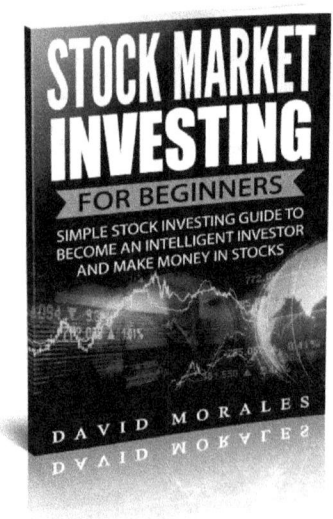

Get More Details Here:

https://mybook.to/stock-investing

www.ingramcontent.com/pod-product-compliance
Lightning Source LLC
Chambersburg PA
CBHW051318220526
45468CB00004B/1400